MEXICAN MILITARISM

The Political Rise and Fall of the Revolutionary Army 1910-1940

MEXICAN

THE POLITICAL RISE AND FALL
OF THE REVOLUTIONARY ARMY

MILITARISM

1910-1940 BY EDWIN LIEUWEN

GREENWOOD PRESS, PUBLISHERS
WESTPORT, CONNECTICUT

Library of Congress Cataloging in Publication Data

Lieuwen, Edwin, 1923-
   Mexican militarism.

   Reprint of the ed. published by University of
New Mexico Press, Albuquerque.
   Bibliography: p.
   Includes index.
   1. Mexico--History--1910-1946. 2. Civil
supremacy over the military--Mexico. 3. Mexico--
Armed Forces--Political activity. I. Title.
[F1234.L69 1981]   972.08'2   80-28937
ISBN 0-313-22911-2 (lib. bdg.)

Due acknowledgment is made to the following books and
publishers from which the illustrations in this book are
drawn: Armin Haab, *Mexican Graphic Art,* New York:
George Wittenborn, Inc., 1957; *La Revolucion Mexicana
vista por Jose Guadalupe Posada,* Mexico City: Talleres
"Policromia," 1960; *Twenty Centuries of Mexican Art,*
New York & Mexico City: The Museum of Modern Art,
1940; *Artes en Mexico,* Numero 45 / Ano XI, 1960.

© The University of New Mexico Press 1968.

Due acknowledgment is made to the following books and
publishers from which the illustrations in this book are
drawn: Armin Haab, *Mexican Graphic Art,* New York:
George Wittenborn, Inc., 1957; *La Revolucion Mexicana
vista por Jose Guadalupe Posada,* Mexico City: Talleres
"Policromia," 1960; *Twenty Centuries of Mexican Art,*
New York & Mexico City: The Museum of Modern Art,
1940; *Artes en Mexico,* Numero 45 / Ano XI, 1960.

Reprinted with the permission of The University of New
Mexico Press.

Reprinted in 1981 by Greenwood Press
A division of Congressional Information Service, Inc.
88 Post Road West, Westport, Connecticut 06881

Printed in the United States of America

10 9 8 7 6 5 4 3 2 1

TABLE OF CONTENTS

CONTENTS

LIST OF ILLUSTRATIONS

MAJOR AREAS OF REVOLUTIONARY
ACTIVITY IN MEXICO

States, when not named, bear the same names as their capitals.

PREFACE

MY Arms and Politics in Latin America (New York, Praeger, 1960) was a pioneering effort to depict the changing role of the military in Latin America. Since 1960, United States academic and government interest in this subject has developed rapidly and has led to a number of other general studies which have refined, revised, and expanded my tentative hypotheses and observations. Continuing interest in this subject led me to the conclusion that only more intensive historical studies of the armed forces in individual countries would yield the kind of data necessary for comparative analysis. To this end, the Rockefeller Foundation provided support to the University of New Mexico for a two-year program of studies on the historical and contemporary role of the armed forces in Latin America.

The program of studies was organized around a graduate seminar directed by the author. Each country undertaken for a project involved a minimum of one year of research in the field. In addition to the present work, five others have been completed: Frederick Nunn (Portland State College) *Civil-Military Relations in Chile, 1891-1938* (Ph.D. Thesis, University of New Mexico, 1963); José Ferrer (Southern Oregon State College) *The Armed Forces in Argentine Politics, 1880-1930* (Ph.D. Thesis, University of New Mexico, 1965); Richard Millett

ix

(Southern Illinois University) *The History of the Guardia Nacional in Nicaragua, 1926-1965* (Ph.D. Thesis, University of New Mexico, 1966); Winfield Burggraaff (University of Missouri) *Civil-Military Relations in Venezuela, 1899-1958* (Ph.D. Thesis, University of New Mexico, 1967); and Robert Elam (University of Massachusetts) *The Military in El Salvador, 1930-1964* (Ph.D. Thesis, University of New Mexico, 1968).

A work by Norman Marin (University of Southern California) on *The Army of the Republic in Brazil (1889-1930)* is in the final stages. Once all the studies have been completed, a comparative historical analysis will be attempted.

The present work is essentially a history of a political process. Is is the story of the seizure of power by the Mexican Army of the Revolution in the years 1910-1914, of the exercise of that power from 1915 to 1935, and of the involuntary surrender of it in the years 1935-1940. It attempts to explain how the old regime and the traditional society were destroyed, and presents both the constructive and destructive features of the military management of the Revolution. It tries to provide some appreciation of just what it takes to mold a revolutionary army of civilian amateurs into a disciplined professional body that shuns politics. And finally, it analyzes how civilian political authority was reestablished in Mexico.

In the preparation of this work I am particularly indebted to John P. Harrison, who, when he served as Associate Director of Humanities for the Rockefeller Foundation, helped structure the study proposal; to Daniel Cosio Villegas and Luis Mora of the Colegio de Mexico, who paved the way for me in Mexico; and to the fine staffs of the National Archives and the Library of Congress in Washington, D.C., and of the Archivo General de la Nación and the Hemeroteca Nacional in Mexico City. Finally, research support from the Ford Foundation has enabled me to complete this book.

E D W I N   L I E U W E N
Albuquerque, New Mexico

INTRODUCTION

MEXICO is unique among the major nations of Latin America today. She is the only nation that has been able to stabilize her politics, modernize her economy, and maintain a modicum of social equilibrium. These achievements are the result of her great social Revolution. The revolutionary experience was one in which the revolutionary army played the dominant role. It destroyed the old regime and the traditional society; it supplied the leadership and the social conscience for building a new government and a new society; and it was the most important political force in Mexico during the critical period from 1910 to 1940.

Prior to the Revolution of 1910, Mexico had suffered long and deeply from militarism. Hundreds of armed uprisings disturbed the internal order of the republic during her initial century of nationhood. Politics was a game played with swords and guns, and the victors, more often than not, claimed the treasury as their spoil. The word "army" became synonymous, in the eyes of civilian political leaders, with crime, venality, violence, and corruption, and Mexico's nineteenth-century historians did not hesitate to attribute much of the nation's political, social, and economic miseries to militarism.

The Revolution of 1910 by no means ended military rule, for although the regular army was destroyed in the process, a revolutionary army was created in its place, the leaders of which dominated Mexican politics for more than a quarter century. No sooner had the Revolution triumphed than the victorious amateur warriors began fighting each other for political power and other spoils of victory. Two years of internecine warfare were necessary before even a modicum of stability could be attained. What is more, the generals of the Revolution often displayed the same rapacious and predatory temperaments which had characterized the regulars they replaced.

The revolutionary army, however, also played a constructive role. In 1917 it was instrumental in giving juridical form to concepts for social reform, and from 1920 to 1935 it became the prime catalyst in the process of social change. The use of force, or at least the threat to use it, apparently was necessary not only for the destruction of the old society but also for the construction of a new one. Even though by 1930 the military's political control was no longer necessary and its social mission had ended, the army was still reluctant to permit civilians to rule Mexico.

The Revolution of 1910 gave rise to a new militarism, but it also released forces which would ultimately result in the triumph of civilian authority. To a considerable extent, the revolutionary chieftains themselves were their own undoing. The quadrennial cycle of presidential succession inevitably produced crises and revolts as each president tried to impose his own successor. The fate of the losers was death, imprisonment, or exile. The 1915-16 struggles eliminated most of the generals loyal to Pancho Villa and Emiliano Zapata; the 1920 rebellion eliminated those who backed Venustiano Carranza; the victors of 1920 in turn eliminated half the active generals in the 1923 uprising and another one-fourth in the rebellions of 1927 and 1929. The losing military politicians, unlike civilians who can try again, were forever ruined politically. By 1929, a cabal of five *divisionarios* (division generals) had become clearly dominant, and Lázaro Cárdenas, a member of the clique, delivered the coup de grace to four of these. He eliminated Plutarco Elías Calles and Joaquín Amaro in 1935, Saturnino Cedillo in 1938, arranged for the electoral defeat of Juan Andreu Almazán in 1940, and then he himself retired, leaving politics to the official party and the civilian bureaucracy.

While the revolutionary generals were destroying each other in internecine warfare, a professional army was being developed. Led by young officers trained in the military academy, the new army concentrated its energies upon the exercise of military functions and eschewed politics. In the critical election of 1940, when the Cárdenas administration challenged the revolutionary generals, the new professional army remained loyal to the government. It required a revolutionary general (Cárdenas) and a new army to break the hold of the revolutionary chieftains.

The decline of the political power of the military was accompanied by the rise of civilian political forces—forces which had been set in motion by the process of social revolution. As Mexico became more stable politically, she began to develop economically, and as social change took place in the aftermath of the Revolution, the personalistic rule of the military chieftains became less and less suited to the increasingly complex political needs of the nation. As a consequence, labor, agrarian, professional and bureaucratic interest groups rose to contest the political monopoly of the revolutionary generals, and in 1929 Calles incorporated these emerging groups into an official party. The army remained supreme inside the party until Cárdenas began watering down its influence by deliberately encouraging the development of civilian counterpoises. He then reorganized the official party in such a way that the military could no longer control it. The elections of 1940 finally ended the political sway of the generals of the Revolution.

MEXICAN MILITARISM

The Political Rise and Fall of the Revolutionary Army 1910-1940

1910·1914

I

THE REVOLUTION

THE DÍAZ REGIME
1876-1910

General Porfirio Díaz was the first ruler in Mexican history to bridle the provincial military chieftains and render them subordinate to the central government. Because the victorious 1876 revolution produced a whole new crop of ambitious generals, many of them greedy and treacherous, it took Díaz nearly fifteen years to achieve full military control.

Machiavellian techniques were utilized to the fullest by Díaz. Rivals too dangerous to confront in battle he pacified with opportunities for graft and plunder. The loyalty of others he purchased with generous salaries and expense accounts. Many were given the opportunity to forfeit their political ambitions in exchange for economic concessions and landed estates.[1]

For those generals who could not be bought, other techniques

1

were applied. Some potential rivals were made military attachés at embassies abroad; others were assigned such bizarre missions as studying the influence of Russian climate upon cavalry operations; still others were relieved of direct command of troops by "promotion" to governorships. Provincial military leaders who declined such honors were deliberately goaded into rebellion, then crushed by superior government forces. Sometimes those who had been granted opportunities for graft would be "exposed," then cashiered from the army on charges of corruption. By such methods Díaz got rid of more than five hundred officers, including one-quarter of his one hundred generals, during the 1880's. To keep the retired loyal, he set up in the War Ministry a Depósito de Jefes y Oficiales (Trust of Chiefs and Officers) where former officers could continue to collect one-half the salary of their last active rank simply by registering.[2]

To insure the loyalty of those on active duty, Díaz divided Mexico into eleven military zones, each of them overlapping various of the twenty-seven states. To the states he appointed civilian governors, and to protect himself against conspiracies amongst governors and zone commanders, he transferred the latter frequently. To prevent an officer from gaining the personal allegiance of any large body of men, he extended this system of shifting commands all the way down to the regimental level.[3] Such was the manner in which Díaz destroyed provincial militarism and developed in its stead a national army that sustained the central government.

The Díaz regime included other important stabilizing features. The dictator obtained the support of the two major civilian political forces which had been at odds throughout Mexico's previous national history. The ecclesiastical and land-holding conservatives were won over by Díaz's policies of protecting traditionalist society and religion, while Liberals were induced to abandon federalism in exchange for the economic benefits of commercial, industrial, and bureaucratic development.[4]

Because the Díaz regime provided few benefits to the masses,

2

the latter had to be controlled by force and terror. Though the army had been built up ostensibly to defend Mexico against foreign threats, it functioned almost exclusively as an internal police force. In urban and mining areas the army did the bidding of the merchants, industrialists, and foreign enterprises by curbing the workers. In the countryside, the masses were rendered docile by the brutality and terrorist methods of the infamous *rurales,* a mounted constabulary corps made up largely of former bandits.[5]

The Díaz system was self-reinforcing. The military provided the order necessary for economic development, and economic development provided the revenues necessary to keep the military loyal. Economic growth also built a modern communications network, which made it far easier for the army to stamp out disorders in outlying areas.

Though a nonprofessional himself, Díaz saw the value of professionalism for improving the capabilities of the army, for developing its esprit de corps, and, very importantly, for divorcing it from politics by keeping it fully occupied with military duties. His models were the French, German, and United States armies. From them he procured such hand-me-down equipment as Franco-Prussian War cannons and Remington rifles. He did not employ foreign military missions, but he sent observers to St. Cyr and West Point, and he adopted the latest European training manuals.[6]

When Díaz seized power, there were no professionals in the Mexican army; there were only those civilian amateurs who had won their military spurs in the War of the Reform (1858-1861) and in the fight against the French Intervention (1862-1867). During the 1880's the dictator established the Chapultepec Military Academy. Selected as cadets were men of "good family," which meant they were white and not of the masses. They pursued four years of technical studies in the arts of modern warfare. Under Díaz, Military Academy enrollments averaged three hundred, with sixty cadets receiving commissions annually. Half the nine thousand officers in the army were graduates of Chapultepec by the turn of the century.[7]

Photographs of the time reveal clean-cut, neatly uniformed, white-skinned youths of good military bearing. Professor Percy Martin observed that the course of instruction at Chapultepec "is a very thorough and efficient one," that the graduates were "fine young fellows...extremely careful of their behavior in public." He was also impressed by their nontechnical training, observing, for example, that most of the young officers "know several foreign languages."[8] Thomas Janvier noted the general efficiency and the high morale. He attributed this to government concern for the officers' welfare, to a fair and orderly promotion system, and to just salary and retirement policies.[9]

This rosy foreign picture of the Díaz army concealed some basic weaknesses from the outside world. For one thing, the theoretical studies pursued at Chapultepec had little relevance to Mexico's military needs. Preparations at the academy were for external defense against some foreign enemy or for imaginary campaigns abroad, whereas the actual tasks of the army were limited to policing functions exclusively inside Mexico. Secondly, nearly all the generals were nonprofessionals and most of them were very old by 1900; thirdly, there was widespread corruption in high military places; and fourthly, the army was incredibly overstaffed. For the nine thousand officers, the table of organization provided for 25,000 enlisted men.[10] But the officers, who received per diem allowances to feed their men, padded their muster rolls by an estimated 40 per cent and pocketed the excess money. Thus, only about eighteen thousand enlisted men, or two per officer, were actually in service.[11]

If the officers were presentable, the rank and file were not. The so-called "volunteer" system was in reality one of forced recruitment, for conditions were such that few men would willingly serve in the ranks. Consequently, vagabonds and beggers were rounded up from the city streets while from the outlying states local politicians would deliver troublesome individuals to the army garrisons. Jails were often emptied to provide troops. Such conscripts felt no pride, but only fear and hatred for the officers. They were garbed shabbily, fed inadequately, trained poorly, and treated badly.[12] When the 1910 Revolution came, many defected at the first opportunity.

When the French were driven from Mexico in 1867, the bonds amongst officers, the men and the common people of Mexico were extremely close, since all had participated in a great national crusade. But the Díaz system broke down these close associations, because it had no place for commoners; instead the army became the tool for the development and preservation of class and institutional privilege. Turn-of-the-century photographs reveal a kind of creole Prussianism—haughty, monocled, white, spit-and-polish officers in command of colored, barefoot, ragged, hungry men. The army mirrored the profound social inequalities of civilian life.[13] The officers were completely out of touch with the soldiers and the common people, and they maltreated and exploited both. Opulent in the midst of poverty, unstinting in its use of brutality, lacking in morality and without social conscience, the officer corps epitomized nearly everything the masses resented under the Díaz system. Small wonder then that it became the object upon which the hate of the revolutionaries was focused.

BACKGROUND TO THE 1910 REVOLUTION

Scholars of revolution have observed that social upheavals are not likely to occur in periods of economic depression and stagnation, for such conditions tend to dampen rather than stimulate political action. Rather, social revolutions are more likely to be the by-products of growing prosperity. This was clearly the case in Mexico, for under Díaz the nation had experienced a full generation of economic development and growing prosperity.

Another characteristic of social revolutions is that they are not sparked by representatives of the masses: the leadership comes from disaffected men of property and disillusioned intellectuals. Mexico's Revolution was initially headed by wealthy individuals who had been denied political opportunity. Francisco Madero, son of a Coahuila *hacendado* (large landholder) rebelled when his political ambitions were thwarted by the exclusivism of the Díaz system. Venustiano Carranza, a prosperous, propertied, provincial politician, joined the Madero uprising because he felt his talents were insufficiently appreciated by Díaz's technocrats in the capital. Also, because the Díaz regime barred him from opportunity in public life, Abraham González, nephew of the governor of Chihuahua and also of prosperous family, joined the Liberal opposition several years before the Revolution began.[14]

The revolutionary fever was apparent several years before the outbreak of major violence in 1910. The opposition activities of the Flores Magón brothers and the labor strikes at Rio Blanco and Cananea are well known. The educated youth, aware that the static character of the Díaz government was unsuited to Mexico's changing needs, increasingly agitated against the dictatorship and founded the antiadministration Ateneo de la Juventud (Youth Atheneum) in 1909.[15]

Once fighting broke out, the Revolution gained support from rising middle-class elements hungry for material gain and political power; from peasants anxious to acquire their own lands; and from bandit and guerrilla hordes who relished the prospect of new and exhilarating experiences.

Ironically, the uprising against Díaz was precipitated by changes brought about by Díaz; for the economic development he fostered was accompanied by social change. In the cities industrialization gave rise to a middle class and an urban proletariat. In rural areas, where living conditions were particularly harsh because land continued to be concentrated in few hands, the rise of leaders like Emiliano Zapata and Pascual Orozco can be partially explained as a consequence of the oppression of the peasantry. The Díaz era also coincided with a significant improvement in the lot of middle-class farmers; yet these *ranch-*

6

eros, of whom Alvaro Obregón was the prototype, nonetheless provided the bulk of the military leadership of the Revolution.

Class antagonisms rose sharply in the decade prior to the Revolution. Urban and mining labor increasingly had to be curbed with troops. The restlessness of the middle groups was also widespread—the *rancheros,* the petty bureaucrats, the lawyers, the teachers, and the *oficiales* (lieutenants and majors). These were all men on the rise economically and socially, men with means above the level of subsistence, men of unrecognized talent, and men whose ambitions were stifled by the inflexible political structure.

Thus the initial stages of a social revolution had already begun before 1910. The new social groups created by the Díaz prosperity were not incorporated into the governing structure to provide the broader national consensus which political stability required after 1900.

Lyford P. Edwards, a pioneer scholar in the sociology of

THE REVOLUTION 1910 1911

revolutions, observed that prior to the outbreak of a social revolution, ferment builds up for years until the political "oppression psychosis" reaches the breaking point. An essential step in reaching this point, he noted, "is the gradual concentration of public dissatisfaction upon some one institution and persons representing it."[16] In Mexico the "institution" was the army, and the "person representing it" was General Porfirio Díaz.

Madero's initial success can be attributed to this focus of hatred upon the common enemy which helped produce a temporary unity amongst the heterogeneous upper-, middle-, and lower-income opposition groups. His *Sucesión Presidential en 1910,* a political tract written in 1908 to enhance his candidacy, concentrates upon the problem of militarism. More than a third of the book is devoted to nineteenth-century army rule in Mexico, the argument being that Mexico's twentieth-century prob-

7

lems were inherited from her militaristic past.[17] He excoriated "selfish and cynical" generals such as Agustín Iturbide, Anastasio Bustamante, and Santa Anna, "who demanded maximum payment for their services." He drew parallels between praetorianism in the Roman Republic and nineteenth-century Mexico. He praised Benito Juárez as the "incarnation of civilism," and lamented the return of army rule in the person of Díaz following Juárez's death.[18]

By the spring of 1910, Madero's initial democratic idealism began to founder in the face of political realities. For he finally realized that Díaz, despite his public assertions, had no intention of permitting free elections. "It will be necessary to start a revolution to otherthrow him," Madero concluded.[19] When Díaz imprisoned Madero on a bogus charge of "disturbing the peace" and then declared himself "reelected," there was nothing left for Madero to do but fight. Escaping from prison in October 1910, he called on the people to rebel. He scheduled the uprising for November 20.[20]

Madero's Plan of San Luis Potosí was an antimilitaristic pronouncement. It stated that the rule of the generals would have to end before democracy could come to Mexico. Since Díaz controlled the regular armed forces, Madero had to create a revolutionary army, the Ejército Libertador, in order to destroy them. The Plan of San Luis Potosí provided that: "(1) the chiefs of the voluntary forces will assume the military grade which corresponds to the number of troops under their command; (2) the military grades of the civilian chiefs who serve out the revolution will be ratified by the Secretary of War when the revolution triumphs."[21] Thus, those who aspired to a career in arms and had been blocked by the Díaz system might see that their wishes could be fulfilled if they participated in a victorious rebellion. Madero also promised promotions to all *federales* (regulars) who would defect to the Ejército Libertador.[22]

Though Madero himself had little fear of physical violence, he hoped the revolution would be relatively bloodless. This was why he invited the *federales* to join his movement. His revolutionary plan called for the strict observance of the laws of warfare, humane treatment of military prisoners, and the outlawing of shrapnel ammunition.[23]

In late October 1910, Madero, then in Texas, sent agents to contact opposition leaders in northern Mexico. In mid-November he again urged the *federales* to defect, simultaneously admonishing them to "remember [that] the mission of the army is to defend institutions and not to be the unconscious support of the tyranny."[24] On November 20, 1910, right on schedule, he crossed the border and proclaimed the beginning of the Revolution.

Things hardly went according to plan. Minor insurrections broke out in half a dozen states; but as these were poorly coordinated the *federales* soon brought them under control; Madero dejectedly returned to Texas. Early in 1911, however, new outbreaks occurred in the north. The one in Chihuahua, led by Pancho Villa and Pascual Orozco, began to gain momentum in February. To crush it, Díaz sent five thousand troops, but the operation failed, and word soon spread that the hitherto invincible *federales* had been defeated.[25]

This sudden revelation of the regime's weakness gave courage to revolutionary bands throughout the republic, and the movement rapidly began to spread. It quickly became apparent that the government lacked sufficient troops to deal with so many uprisings at once, and Madero was soon back in Mexico attempting to direct operations. On May 10, 1911, Ciudad Juárez fell, and shortly thereafter Díaz capitulated.

What explains the sudden triumph of the Madero rebellion? Victors always attribute their success to their own heroic deeds and superior fighting abilities. And it is true, considering the motley recruits comprising the Ejército Libertador (peasants, laborers, farmers, shopkeepers, students, and professional men), and considering their assortment of weapons (machetes, pistols, sticks, stones, and rifles), that the military achievement of these citizen soldiers appears remarkable.[26] What happened in the

9

spring of 1911 was that armed bands under self-appointed chiefs arose all over the republic, drove Díaz officials from the vicinity, seized government offices, money, and stamps, and staked out spheres of local authority. Towns and cities, as well as the countryside, passed to the control of the Maderistas.[27]

These rebel bands were generally formed into companies. Nearly all the troops were mounted, and a goodly number—thanks to effective smuggling—were equipped with 30-30 Winchester rifles. The rebels had the further advantage of operating on friendly ground; they knew the terrain, could live off the country, and thus were not forced to maintain long supply lines.[28]

Since only about one hundred days elapsed between the February revolutionary outbreak, and the May collapse of the Díaz regime, the fighting phase of the rebellion does not seem very important.[29] Considering the small number of battles actually fought, triumph was more directly attributable to the weakness of the *federales* than to the strength of the Ejército Libertador.

Indeed, the Federal Army was weak and decrepit by 1910. There was no professional office for strategy and planning; instead, the War Ministry staff was a corrupt bureaucracy jockeying for favors and position. Díaz himself played politics with the army. Over fifty per cent of the conscripts were illiterate Indians; the remainder were vagabonds, beggars, and criminals, and the army command made no effort to improve the health, military bearing or habits of these troops. The men were given minimal training in the use of firearms and were seldom taken on maneuvers or exercises. The non-coms, whose main qualification was an ability to read and write, were demoralized by the corruption, irresponsibility, and indifference of the officers.[30]

Upon graduation most young officers would begin their career-long search for economic, rather than military, opportunities. The most coveted rank was that of *jefe* (colonel), nicknamed *las buscas* (perquisites), a rank which entitled one to pad the muster roles and graft on food and supplies. And when a *jefe's* conduct became sufficiently scandalous, his punishment was apt to be promotion to *brigadier* (brigadier general). The rank of *divisionario* (division general), however, was reserved to the heroes of the 1862-1867 wars against the French. All the *divisionarios* were over seventy by 1910.[31]

When the Maderistas finally forced the *federales* to take the field, the latter's ineffectiveness surprised even those who had known of their deficiencies. Supply lines broke down almost immediately; shoddy European armaments functioned poorly; and the National Arms Factory proved incapable of producing monthly more than 15,000 shells, about a half day's supply. Twelve thousand troops, only half the number on the muster rolls, were ready for field action in February 1911, but Díaz dared commit only a fraction of these to the main trouble area in Chihuahua lest the capital itself become vulnerable to attack. Instead he mainly relied on his ten thousand *rurales* to conduct a holding action in the north until more conscripts could be pressed into service.[32] When confronted with battle, however, the wretched conscripts "deserted in droves."[33]

11

The Díaz regime collapsed because the army was incapable of defending it. Díaz himself was responsible for the inept management and poor organization of the army, and for permitting it to diminish from 35,000 in 1900 to 20,000 in 1910, a time when changing social conditions required an expanding military organization.[34]

1911 **MADERO AND THE** Under the Treaty of Ciu-
1913 **MILITARY PROBLEM** dad Juárez (May 21, 1911), Díaz resigned the presidency, Madero renounced his claim to the provisional presidency, and Foreign Secretary Francisco de la Barra was designated interim president pending general elections in October 1911.[35] In the interest of ending hostilities, Madero agreed to discharge the rebel forces in central and southern Mexico, provided that those revolutionaries (who so desired) in Sonora, Coahuila, and Chihuahua be incorporated into a new military force to be known as the Cuerpos Rurales de la Federación. Thus the task of preserving internal order remained primarily with the old Federal Army.[36]

Although Madero made this compromise for the noblest of reasons, his decision sowed the seeds of future military troubles. For the Ciudad Juárez Treaty violated the Plan of San Luis Potosí proviso that permanent military rank be awarded to all who joined the Revolution. Rebel officers were not the only ones chagrined at the loss of the spoils of victory, for many in the ranks also fought for personal gain. Yet the Ciudad Juárez Treaty obviously favored the *federales*.

When the *federales* were made responsible for the protection of the new government, Madero's associates protested that these regulars actually were enemies of the Revolution. Madero, however, felt that the main enemy was Díaz, and now that he had been eliminated, militarism would disappear and civilian authority would prevail.[37]

Toward the end of June, only a month after the triumph of the rebellion, President de la Barra began discharging the revolutionaries. He attempted to assuage them with six million pesos in bonuses and with pensions for the wounded.[38] A number of revolutionary generals, led by Francisco Vásquez Gómez, demanded permanent rank as provided by the Plan of San Luis Potosí, but Madero condemned them for insubordination to civilian authority.[39]

De la Barra decreed on June 30 that any revolutionary who resisted discharge be considered a bandit.[40] As a result of such stern policies and the support Madero gave them, most of the revolutionaries were mustered out by the end of July. By August 1911, Mexico's armed forces consisted of sixteen thousand *federales* and twelve thousand from the Ejército Libertador. And half of the latter were scheduled for an early discharge.[41] All did not go smoothly, however. The bonuses were not paid promptly and the pension system was managed badly. Some revolutionaries, distrustful of the government, such as the Zapatistas in Morelos, refused to lay down their arms.[42]

Former members of the Ejército Libertador had good grounds for suspicion, for while de la Barra was dealing harshly with revolutionaries, he was favoring the *federales,* including some of the more notorious partisans of the Díaz regime.[43] As the protests swelled, Madero called for more patience in dealing with the revolutionary bands, and he further incurred the wrath of the *federales* by criticizing General Victoriano Huerta's attacks upon the Zapatistas. During the presidential campaign, he made conspiracy charges against Generals Huerta and Bernardo Reyes. During September 1911 the United States Embassy reported that while the morale of the army was good and its concept of honor high, it "is unquestionably hostile to Madero, who through want of tact, has said uncomplimentary things about it."[44]

In this troubled atmosphere elections were held in early October 1911. Although Madero was the overwhelming choice over de la Barra and Emilio Vásquez Gómez, by the time he was inaugurated on November 6 his strength had been greatly eroded during the five months since his revolutionary triumph.

13

De la Barra had made use of the interim presidency to strengthen antirevolutionary forces, both military and civilian, while Madero's own stand, particularly with respect to demobilization, had created disunity in the revolutionary ranks. As a consequence, Madero was plagued by pressures both from the right and left throughout his entire fifteen months in the presidency. Charles Cumberland averred that "on no single day was the country at full peace under him."[45]

Inherited from de la Barra was the Zapata problem. While Madero continued to plead for patience and the rule of law, the impatient peasants in southern Mexico continued fighting the *federales* and seizing land. Less than three weeks after Madero took office, Zapata abandoned him completely. On November 25, 1911, he issued his Plan of Ayala, which recognized General Pascual Orozco in Chihuahua as the Chief of the Liberating Revolution and declared as traitors all revolutionaries who continued to support Madero.[46] As agrarian violence spread into the states of Puebla, Guerrero, Tlaxcala, and México, President Madero was forced to employ the *federales* to fight his former followers. Yet despite the best efforts of the Federal Army, the Zapatista rebellion continued throughout Madero's presidency.

Madero was also plagued by continuous threats from the right. Only two days after the inauguration, two Federal Army generals were arrested for planning a coup. A month later General Bernardo Reyes attempted a counterrevolution. After the Madero revolution, Reyes decided to remain in the army, but Gustavo Madero, the president's brother, thwarted his bid for a top post. As a consequence, Reyes left for Texas to plan a rebellion. In early December he entered Coahuila at the head of an armed band. Pro-Reyes sentiment, however, was nonexistent in the north despite growing disillusionment with Madero. As a consequence, the *federales* had little difficulty overcoming and imprisoning Reyes by the end of 1911.[47]

On March 3, 1912, General Pascual Orozco launched an uprising in Chihuahua. Historians have customarily attributed this outbreak to the personal animosity of Orozco toward Madero for the niggardly military rewards and honors he received for his brilliant role in the 1910 uprising. Orozco is generally depicted as the dupe of the rightist opposition to Madero. For example, the machinations of the Terrazas family, the greatest landholders in Chihuahua, have been detected in the background in support of Orozco. Also lending weight to this counterrevolutionary thesis is the defection of a number of Federal garrisons to Orozco's banner, and Orozco's later association with General Victoriano Huerta after his own rebellion had failed. Placing this movement in clearer perspective is a recent piece of scholarship by Michael C. Meyer, who demonstrates the genuine revolutionary idealism of Orozco, his bitter disillusionment over Madero's failure to fulfill the promises contained in the Plan of San Luis Potosí, and his close identification with the agrarian revolutionaries under Zapata in the south.[48] Also, although many *federales* fought under Orozco, the great bulk of them fought against his movement. Orozco's main supporters were former revolutionary soldiers, principally those who resented the government's demobilization policies.[49]

The Orozco rebellion proved a most formidable threat to Madero. To meet it he doubled the Federal Army to sixty thousand and sent six thousand men northward under General José González Salas. When Orozco routed this army, Madero sent in General Victoriano Huerta with nine thousand men. Even so, it took five months of hard fighting to crush the Orozco rebellion.[50]

The motives of the October 1912 Veracruz uprising led by General Felix Díaz (Porfirio's nephew) were quite clear. This was a case of opportunistic militarism pure and simple. The Plan Felicista appealed to "the noble army" and to "the sons of the glorious Colegio Militar" to join in "energetic protest against the tyrannical Madero government." Felix Díaz urged the army to assume responsibility for restoring "peace and justice" to Mexico.[51] Initially, the Federal generals wavered in their loyal-

15

ties toward Madero. General Joaquín Beltrán, in command of three thousand troops, hesitated a long time before giving battle to Díaz's army of only a thousand. Ultimately, the *federales* decided to back Madero, and by the end of October, Felix Díaz was defeated, captured, and imprisoned.[52]

The Federal Army officers brought the Madero regime to an end in February 1913. The growing rightist and leftist resistance to the regime and continuing revolutionary violence in the countryside convinced Mexico's conservatives that Madero would have to go. Clerical, business, landholding, and foreign investor elements urged the generals to oust the President, while Felix Díaz and Bernardo Reyes plotted from their cells.[53]

The February 9, 1913, *cuartelazo* (barracks coup), the subsequent ten-days battle in the streets of Mexico City, and the intervention of United States Ambassador Henry Lane Wilson to help install General Victoriano Huerta in the presidency, is a story too well known to warrant retelling here. Suffice it to say that Madero was betrayed by the Federal officers in whom he had placed his trust, was removed from office by them, imprisoned and then assassinated by them.[54]

Why did Madero fail? González Ramírez feels that the Federal officers planned to destroy him from the outset, that they were actually abetted in their opposition to him by revolutionary generals like Zapata and Orozco, and that when the latter two were brought under control, the *federales* were then free to launch their coup.[55] Juan Barragán's explanation of Madero's failure is simply that "the new government didn't govern with the revolutionaries" and that, accordingly, "counterrevolution was a natural and logical result."[56] Cumberland declares, however, that "the thesis that the demobilization of the rebel army was responsible for Madero's fall is untenable, for there was no assurance that the revolutionary army, of sufficient strength to attack the Federals, would not attack the government." More significant, he believes, is the fact that "Madero's refusal to pander to military men, both regular and irregular, made him unpopular with the majority in the army."[57]

And yet it is doubtful that Madero could have survived even if he had cultivated better relations with the armed forces. For it is generally futile for a ruler to attempt to control, by gentle tactics, a praetorian army. Yet, if Madero had refrained from public criticism of his prominent generals, such as Miguel Mondragón and Victoriano Huerta, for their inability to account for certain funds or for their alleged mistakes in the field, perhaps he might have survived a while longer.

Madero's inability to implement the political principles for which his revolution stood and to provide a viable government for Mexico certainly stemmed directly from his inability to control the military, either the *federales* or the revolutionaries. But it is significant that there was an insufficient anti-Madero consensus amongst the revolutionary groups to oust the President, and such a consensus did exist amongst the *federales*. When the latter brought the Madero regime to an end, however, it meant that Mexico's half-way revolution could no longer continue. It had to be either completed or destroyed. In the next sixteen months of battle, the issue as to who was going to govern Mexico, the *federales* or the revolutionaries, was finally to be decided.

THE CONSTITUTION- Gen. Victoriano Huerta's
1913 **ALIST ARMY VERSUS** coup d'etat was a counter-
1914 **THE FEDERAL ARMY** revolution. Though primarily a military undertaking, it was a movement in which the Church, the large landholders, and the business interests, both foreign and domestic, rejoiced. The Madero interlude had threatened the civilian right, and they were perfectly content to have the Federal Army assume political power in order to get protection against the left.

Although it was relatively easy for Huerta to take Mexico City, it was quite another matter to restore the Díaz system to the countryside. In an attempt to do so, Huerta appointed Federal generals to replace the Maderista governors and deployed troops to occupy the various states.

Revolutionary writers have been extremely harsh in describing Huerta's rule. They emphasize his brutality, his excessive drinking, and his irresponsibility in governing. But the revolutionaries were no more humane than the *federales*. Both shot prisoners and committed rape. On June 30, 1913, United States Ambassador Henry Lane Wilson reported that "fifty women of good family in Durango committed suicide following capture of the city and being ravished by the rebel soldiers." At year's end John Lind reported from Veracruz that "after six months of warfare, there is not one Constitutionalist commander in Federal prison. The explanation is that all those captured have been shot."[58] The brutality on both sides is explained by the fact that Huerta's rule coincided with all-out war between the *federales* and the revolutionaries. This time, in contrast to the 1910 uprising, it was understood there would be no compromise: the

18

vanquished would have to pay with their lives. In any conflict of this nature, brutality and atrocities are apt to be widespread, but they emanated from the situation itself rather than from Huerta's alleged sadism.

The portrait of Huerta as an inebriated madman is also inaccurate. There is no evidence that his drinking interfered with the making of logical decisions. His public speeches reveal an articulate man who firmly believed that the nation must be run by "Mexico's most virtuous, patriotic and honorable institution," namely, the Federal Army.[59] Huerta did not fail because of his stupidity, his alcoholism, or his ineptitude—he failed because the military resources at his command were unequal to those in opposition.

Although Huerta claimed to have 68,400 men—25,000 regulars, 31,000 state militia, and 12,400 *rurales*—it is doubtful that he ever had as many of fifty thousand. González Ramírez notes that the *federales* did not outnumber the revolutionaries in a single major battle and that the Federal Army numbered less than forty thousand in August 1914.[60] In addition, Huerta's task was made doubly difficult by the fact that the Madero revolution had not only destroyed Díaz's political control system, but had also placed large quantities of arms in the hands of irregular bands. Add to this the United States' arming of the revolutionaries while blocking arms shipments to the *federales*, and Huerta's defeat would appear inevitable.

But in the final analysis, Huerta failed to defeat Carranza's Constitutionalist Army for the same reason Díaz failed to defeat Madero's Liberation Army. The chief weakness of the Federal Army was still the poor quality of its troops. For Huerta still had to rely on the infamous *leva* (draft). This meant forceful induction of criminals, vagabonds, and beggars in the cities and Indian peons in the countryside. Lind reported how the poor people feared coming into the streets for fear of being "recruited"; "some 'volunteers' are captured in Mexico City but most are brought in from the country districts. Squads of soldiers are sent out in all directions with coils of rope hanging from their saddles, and peons who are sighted are roped and marched or transported to the nearest *cuartel*."[61]

Small wonder that the ranks of the *federales,* where the men were little more than armed slaves, were constantly depleted by mutinies and desertions. They had little concept of fighting for either a cause or their country.[62] A month after the Constitutionalist Revolution broke out, the United States Military Attaché in Mexico City reported: "the government has less than eight thousand efficient troops on which it can count as loyal."[63]

The men in the Constitutionalist Army, on the other hand, generally had something to fight for. Though their leaders often tried to instill in them a high sense of political, social, and patriotic mission, the prospect of personal gain counted for a good deal more. Many who joined Carranza were disgruntled revolutionaries who had fought under Madero and were subsequently mustered out against their will. Although the most articulate anti-Huerta elements were urban, the Constitutionalist ranks were filled by men of rural origin, by men who attacked with vengeance the *federales,* the *rurales* and the *hacendados* who had enslaved them for so long. There were some revolutionary troops of urban origin, but they were poor horsemen and inept at surviving in the countryside.[64]

The differences in the morale and fighting quality of the officer corps were not so marked. Madero's revolution had rooted out many of the incompetents from the Federal Army. The officers who battled Reyes, Orozco, Zapata, and Felix Díaz in 1911-1912 gave fair accounts of themselves. That their technical abilities were valued is demonstrated by the willingness with which Constitutionalist forces accepted the services of Federal defectors, such as General Felipe Angeles, who served as Carranza's sub-Secretary of War; Colonel Luis Medina Barrón, who advanced to *divisionario* rank after fighting for the Constitutionalist Army; and Captain Eugenio Martínez, who also became a general after training Obregón's first company of troops.[65] Though nearly all the Federal officers were professionals graduated from the Chapultepec Academy, some revolutionaries who originally fought for Madero in 1910, such as Pascual Orozco, became officers in the Federal Army during its fight against the Constitutionalists.[66] And the Cedillo brothers of San Luis Potosí might have fought for Huerta had he not insisted on incorporating them and their guerrilla-bandit forces into the regular army.[67]

As in the Madero revolution of 1910, the Constitutionalist officers were amateurs in military matters and of middle-class social origin. Juan Barragán was a student, Alvaro Obregón a *ranchero* and farm machinery salesman, Plutarco Elías Calles a schoolteacher, Francisco Murguía a photographer, Salvador Alvarado a druggist, and Lucio Blanco a stock man. All these men became brilliant revolutionary generals. A few important revolutionary generals had humbler backgrounds, such as Francisco L. Urquizo, who had been an enlisted man in 1910, and Panfilo Natero, an Indian peon who began fighting for Madero.[68] Many revolutionary officers had learned to fight under Madero in

1910-1911. Some of these subsequently gained military experience as members of the Cuerpos Rurales in the years 1911-1913. Others, without previous experience, such as Obregón, simply displayed a natural talent for soldiering.[69]

The origins of the Constitutionalist Army can be traced to the death of Madero. "His martyrdom," wrote Stanley R. Ross, "accomplished what he had been unable to do while alive: unite all the revolutionists under one banner."[70] The creator of the Constitutionalist Army was Coahuila Governor Venustiano Carranza. He condemned Huerta's seizure of power and quickly incorporated the Cuerpos Rurales, all of them veterans of Madero's 1910 revolution, into his rebel army. Aware that he possessed little military talent himself, Carranza left the fighting to others. He refused to take formal military rank; instead he assumed the title *Primer Jefe* (commander-in-chief) and wore civilian garb.[71] In fact, Carranza's whole movement hewed to a civilian thesis. Civilian supremacy, he maintained, could only be achieved by destroying the *federales* and forming a new democratic army which would support "Constitutionalism."[72]

Though Carranza was no fighting general, he did succeed in establishing a unified command in the north and in setting up a military organization capable of beating the *federales*. Both Villa's bands in Chihuahua and Obregón's forces in Sonora agreed, on April 18, 1913, to fight under Carranza. Although Zapata did not recognize Carranza as *Primer Jefe,* he nonetheless contributed to the defeat of the common enemy, the Federal Army.[73]

Carranza promulgated his revolutionary plan at the hacienda of Guadalupe, Coahuila, on March 26, 1913. Here a hundred newly appointed revolutionary officers declared Huerta's assumption of power illegal, refused to recognize any government officials appointed by Huerta, formally created the Ejército Constitutionalista, appointed Carranza *Primer Jefe* of that organization, and designated Carranza provisional president once the Constitutionalist Army had triumphed.[74]

That triumph took a year and a half, from the time of the

February 1913 clash of the revolutionaries with Federal troops, the day after Madero's murder, to formal surrender of the Federal Army. The military history of that struggle is not properly a part of this study. What happened after Carranza denounced Huerta was that an improvised army made up of irregulars, bandits, guerrillas, and volunteers, began to form. From Coahuila the movement spread to Chihuahua, Sonora, Zacatecas and Durango. Within a short time the entire north was under the control of the revolutionaries. These successes gave encouragement to the center and south, so that Zapata's movement not only expanded greatly, but nearly every state in the nation soon sprouted rebel movements.[75]

These improvised armies initially had very limited resources, but by theft and ambush, they acquired guns and ammunition from the *federales*. Originally, nearly all rebel forces consisted of mounted marauding bands; later they developed into more formal organizations including mixed groups of cavalry and infantry.

The Constitutionalist Army was thus a guerrilla army, expert in hit-and-run tactics, assassination, and thievery. Carranza never developed an army capable of challenging the *federales* in open battle. Instead, the *constitucionalistas* simply wore down and chewed up the Federal Army in guerrilla warfare. In this kind of fighting the *federales* were severely hampered by their transport and supply system. They seldom dared operate far from railroad lines, so the *constitucionalistas* tore up the lines, disabled the locomotives, then carried out their raids at will. The Federal Army showed rather good defensive capabilities, but almost no capacity for pursuing their enemy. This was largely because during marches they generally suffered widespread desertions. The revolutionaries forced the *federales* to fight their type of war. They refused to engage in open battle, never attacked strongly defended positions. Rather, they employed ambush, sabotage, and harassment tactics whenever Huerta's forces attempted to move.[76]

The beginning of the end came in the spring of 1914 when

Huerta's problems with the United States were added to the attrition of the Federal Army. When President Woodrow Wilson raised the United States arms embargo, it meant foreign arms for the *constitucionalistas* but none for the *federales*. This finally enabled the *constitucionalistas* to take the offensive in the early summer of 1914. Huerta fled the country on July 15, whereupon Carranza and his armies demanded surrender and demobilization of the entire Federal Army, still nearly forty thousand strong.

War Minister General Francisco S. Carbajal offered Federal Army support to Carranza's government against the Zapatistas, who were then threatening the capital from the south. But Carranza was wise enough not to repeat Madero's mistake. He insisted upon unconditional surrender. General Obregón arranged this. On August 11, 1914, he descended upon Mexico City with forty thousand troops. At the time, the *constitucionalistas* had another fifty-five thousand in reserve in the north. On August 13, General Obregón signed the Treaty of Teoloyucan with Federal General José Refugio. Under its terms the *federales* surrendered all their arms and military installations. The officers and men agreed either to return to civilian pursuits or leave the country.[77] These terms were generally carried out in the last two weeks of August. On August 18, Carranza, with the principal revolutionary chiefs at his side, made his triumphal entry into Mexico City.

Mexico's old-style militarism had thus been utterly destroyed, but what was not yet realized was that a new type of militarism had been developed in its stead. The revolutionary army had liberated the nation from its traditional exploiters and rulers. The burning question soon became: who was going to liberate the nation from its liberators? This was a process that was destined to take a full quarter century, whereas the Revolution itself, from Madero's initial uprising to Carranza's ultimate triumph, had consumed less than four years.

1914·1920

II

THE CÁRRÁNZÁ ERÁ

THE AGUASCALIENTES
CONVENTION
OCTOBER-NOVEMBER 1914

With the surrender and demobilization of the *federales,* political power in Mexico rested in the hands of 150,000 armed revolutionaries. Those entering Mexico City sacked business places,
looted homes, and gunned down policemen. A shocked conservative lamented: "The armed citizen was the only true citizen of
the republic; all others were denied citizenship rights . . . all
institutional, political, economic, and moral rights disappeared
before the exclusive claims of these armed citizens; . . . the
revolutionary warrior caste, in the name of human rights, im-
posed its own terror, law, liberty and justice."[1]

The political exclusivism of the revolutionary leaders is understandable. Since they had won, they felt it was not only their

privilege but their duty to take charge of politics. To them, civilian politicians were unfit to rule,[2] and, the generals exhibited open hostility toward all civilians. General Obregón, during his campaign, repeatedly complained of the cowards and slackers who failed to take up arms against Huerta, and General Francisco Coss, in command of the Puebla area, declared: "When the military united to attack the enemies of the republic the civilians didn't help; therefore, we don't want the civilians to participate in matters of government now."[3]

Though united in the conviction that they alone had the right to govern, the revolutionary generals were by no means in agreement as to who should be president. The principal competitors were Carranza and General Pancho Villa, whose army of forty thousand men was then the most powerful in Mexico. When the Constitutionalist Army was formed, Villa had accepted Carranza as his superior only reluctantly and provisionally. During the fighting Villa often acted independently, and by the time Huerta fled in July 1914, the schism between Villa and Carranza was nearly complete. Involved was personal ambition—both wanted to be president—and ideology—Villa was a radical while Carranza was a moderate. The Villa-Carranza split was reflected in various state struggles—in Sonora between Villista Governor José María Maytorena and Carrancista General Plutarco Elías Calles and in Durango between Villista General Tomás Urbina and the Carrancista Arrieta brothers.

In addition, there was the Zapatista problem. Though Zapata had fought Huerta, he had not collaborated with the Constitutionalist Army. Zapata mistrusted Carranza because the latter was a large landholder. He rejected Carranza's legalism and continued to seize private properties. His peasant army of 25,000 was aided in the field by former *federales* such as Generals Higinio Aguilar, Rafael Eguía Lis, and Benjamín Argumedo.[4]

The August 1914 collapse of the central government precipitated the struggle amongst the leaders of the Revolution. Carranza, aware of Villa's ambitions, ordered Obregón to proceed with all haste to occupy the capital. Meanwhile, he slowed Villa's southward advance by cutting off the coal supply for his lo-comotives. This enabled Obregón's Northwestern Division to reach Mexico City first and to arrange for the surrender of the Federal Army. Five days later, on August 18, Carranza himself arrived, presumably to organize a provisional government along the lines stipulated in the Plan of Guadalupe.

But Carranza's actions now indicated that he intended to be-come more than merely provisional ruler. For example, he did not assume the title of provisional president, since this would make him ineligible for the permanent office. Instead he estab-lished martial law, and was curiously silent about elections. But the thing that worried the Villistas most was Carranza's Septem-ber call to the leading revolutionary chieftains (which by Car-ranza's definition included only Carrancistas) to discuss prob-lems of forming a permanent government. When Villa coun-tered by threatening to rebel, Carranza sent Obregón north to negotiate. The result, much to Carranza's chagrin, was an agree-ment to hold a convention of all military leaders on October 10, 1914, in the neutral city of Aguascalientes.[5]

All the same, the previously planned meeting of Carrancista leaders was held in Mexico City from October 1 to 5. This gath-ering revealed a sharp cleavage between Carranza's civilian and military supporters. The *Primer Jefe* continued to hew to his civilian thesis. He believed that civilian professional men, prin-cipally lawyers, were the best qualified to govern, and appar-ently envisioned himself as president, advised by a civilian cab-inet and congress, with the whole governing structure sustained by a nonpolitical army. The generals, of course, insisted they were far better qualified to govern than such top Carrancista lawyers as Luis Cabrera and Adolfo de la Huerta. Obregón, in particular, the leader of the military sector, tended to equate ci-vilians with trouble-making and even expressed doubts about their patriotism. Incensed, Cabrera charged "the battle has al-ready begun between the new militarism and the constant *ci-vilismo*. . . . I insist that the military must not go alone to Aguascalientes. The generals hold that only the 150,000 armed soldiers should be represented while I believe that the fifteen million Mexicans should have a voice there as well."[6] But words were poor defense against weapons, and so the decision was made that only military men should represent the Carrancistas.

Assembled at Aguascalientes by October 26 were 115 Carracistas, 37 Villistas, and 26 Zapatistas. The qualifications for a delegate were command of at least one thousand troops. After much debate the revolutionary chieftains agreed that, in the interests of peace, both Carranza and Villa should give up their claims to the presidency. Thereupon, a relatively minor revolutionary figure, General Eulalio Gutiérrez of San Luis Potosí, was chosen provisional president. But Villa made no move to withdraw, and Carranza refused to resign the presidency. Ultimatums were exchanged; Gutiérrez was powerless to mediate; Villa began to move his troops toward the capital; Obregón assembled an army to stop him. On November 13 the convention broke up. Civil war was about to begin.

November 1914 August 1915

INTERNECINE WARFARE

Robert Quirk concludes that "Obregón's decision to forsake the Convention and remain with [Carranza] was one of the most decisive acts of the revolution."[7] This move ultimately meant that the Revolution was saved from the extremist leadership of Villa and Zapata. If social origin can be correlated with social identification, then Villa and Zapata were the revolutionary leaders most representative of the Mexican masses. Both were men of humble birth and background, whereas Carranza was an *hacendado* and Obregón a middle-class *ranchero*. However, all four men were motivated by a mixture of personal ambition and revolutionary idealism.

Carranza, according to General Juan Barragán, his most loyal defender, was not only the *Primer Jefe* but also the *Primer Reformista*. In his *Historia del Ejército Constitucionalista*, he claims that Carranza initiated the first genuine agrarian reform in the Mexican revolution on August 29, 1913, when he divided

30

up the Los Borregos hacienda near Matamoros and presented the titles to the peons. And the following month, in an address to the Sonora revolutionaries, Carranza called not only for agrarian reform but also for improved education and living standards for all. These gestures, Barragán maintains, were but the logical preludes to Carranza's January 1915 agrarian and labor reform decrees.[8]

Most revolutionary scholars, however, doubt Carranza's sincerity in behalf of social reform. They feel his upper-class background made him phychologically incapable of identifying with the proletariat; they explain the 1915 decrees as a desperate, opportunistic move to get mass support when he was in danger of being crushed by Villa; and they note that the revolutionary reforms incorporated into the 1917 Constitution remained a dead letter during Carranza's presidency.

In the case of Villa, personal ambition seemed stronger than revolutionary idealism. Villa failed to make use of his powerful political position to launch social reforms. Significantly, the foreign business community preferred Villa to Carranza, Obregón or Zapata.

Though Obregón was also extremely ambitious, his zeal for reform was genuine. During 1915, his labeling of Villa as a reactionary can be dismissed as propaganda but his levies upon the clergy and the business community cannot, since these were moves to improve the lot of urban labor. To the propertied interests in the capital on March 2, 1915, he threatened: "At the first attempt at riot I will leave the city at the head of my troops in order that they might not fire a single shot against the hungry multitude."[9] And Obregón's subsequent break with Carranza involved deep-seated differences in social philosophy.

The most genuine and selfless of the revolutionary leaders was Zapata. He was a true representative of the oppressed classes, and his Indian charges of southern Mexico were the most radical of all the revolutionaries. He had been in constant rebellion, from 1910 till the time of his death at the hands of Carranza's agents in 1919, against the regimes which he felt failed to fulfill their revolutionary promises.[10] But Zapata had little capacity for national leadership. He was uneducated; his horizons were limited to his home region, and his reforms were limited to redistribution of land to the peons.

When the fighting began in late 1914 the Villistas outnumbered the Carrancistas 72,000 to 57,000. In the Villista camp were forty thousand in his Division of the North, 25,000 in Zapata's armies in Morelos and Guerrero, and seven thousand in Panfilo Natera's First Division in north-central Mexico. Carranza could count on 22,000 from Obregón's Army of the Northwest, seven thousand from Pablo González's Northeast Division, ten thousand from Manuel Diéguez in Jalisco, six thousand from Cándido Aguilar in Veracruz, seven thousand from the Arrieta brothers in Durango, and five thousand from General Maclovio Herrera.[11]

Much personal opportunism was displayed during the Carranza-Villa wars. Herrera broke with Villa just before the fighting began, and Generals Lucio Blanco, Rafael Buelna and Juan G. Cabral defected to the new Convention government of Gutiérrez. But once Villa arrived in the capital other *convencion-*

ista generals defected to Carranza. Junior officers often advanced rapidly in rank by alternately offering their services to rival factions. The case of Colonel Cecilio Luna is illustrative. At the time he was finally killed in Villa's 1916 raid on Columbus, New Mexico, the papers in his wallet revealed he had fought for Madero against Díaz, for Orozco against Madero, for Obregón against Orozco, for Hill against Huerta, for Maytorena against Hill, for for Villa against Obregón.[12]

Many *federales* took advantage of the Villa-Carranza wars to attempt a comeback. In addition to those generals fighting for Zapata, General Felipe Angeles and several other ex- *federales* of lesser rank (plus over fifteen hundred Federal enlisted men) fought for Villa. Carranza would have nothing to do with the Federal officers but recruited several thousand former Federal enlisted men. Their services were especially important to the Carrancista armies of Generals Francisco Coss and Cesario Castro.[13]

As Villa and Zapata converged upon the capital after the Aguascalientes Convention broke up, Obregón was obliged to evacuate the remains of the Constitutionalist Army eastward to Veracruz. In early December 1914, provisional President Gutiérrez occupied the National Palace, but Villa and Zapata held the power in Mexico City. The Zapatistas took Puebla in mid-December, but could advance no farther eastward. Villa dared not advance on Veracruz for fear that the Carrancistas (Generals Antonio I. Villarreal and Maclovio Herrera in the north and Manuel Diéguez, Francisco Murguía, and Gertrudis Sánchez in the west), would seize Mexico City. Early in 1915, however, the reorganized Constitutionalist forces in Veracruz, led by Obregón, advanced toward the capital. They took Puebla, whereupon Zapata's army began to disintegrate. Gutiérrez's Conventionist forces then broke with Villa and fled northward, but they were pursued and defeated by the Villistas.[14] The issue would now be decided in a battle between the two titans, Obregón and Villa.

As Villa withdrew northward to prepare for battle, Obregón

occupied Mexico City on January 28, 1915, and began to recruit workers. In early April, the two armies, each twenty thousand strong, converged at Celaya. Here the bloodiest battle in Mexico's history took place. Never before were there attacks of such ferocity or magnitude. Obregón's tactical superiority won the day. Utilizing barbed wire and trench-warfare tactics then being employed in Western Europe, his sharpshooters broke the mass cavalry charges with which Villa had heretofore overwhelmed his opposition. Villa lost seven thousand men in three days. He retreated to the northwest to rebuild and regroup, and two months later Villa and Obregón fought a second major battle at León. As Villa had learned nothing from the first disaster, the outcame was the same.

1915 **CARRANZA AND THE** The victories at Celaya
1919 **MILITARY PROBLEM** and León made it a simple matter for the Carrancistas to retake Mexico City from the Zapatistas in August 1915. Although the Carrancistas thereafter held it permanently, the Villistas and Zapatistas reverted to guerrilla warfare and harassed the Carranza government for another four years. In fact, Carranza had much the same problem as Madero. He had won the revolution and become president of the nation, but his tenure in office was plagued by almost constant rebel disturbances in the countryside.

During the latter half of 1915 and all of 1916, Villa was the principal irritant. Since the Villistas were no longer paid by the government, they turned to banditry, looting, and extortion in the northern states, where policing was poor and governmental control nominal. Irked by United States recognition and support of Carranza, twenty-five Villista generals declared war on the United States in February 1916. This, plus the January execution of sixteen United States engineers and the March 1916 assault on Columbus, New Mexico, resulted in a United States punitive expedition, led by General John J. Pershing, against Villa. For nearly a year, the Carranza government, because of its inability to handle the problem, had to suffer the humiliation of having ten thousand foreign troops on its soil.[15]

But Villa was only the worst of Carranza's many problems. In early 1917, while Villa continued his activities in Chihuahua and Durango, the Cedillo brothers ruled large sections of San Luis Potosí and Coahuila; Veracruz was divided amongst bandit chieftains Manuel Pelaez, Higinio Aguilar, and the Márquez brothers, who conducted frequent forays into Puebla and Oaxaca; and the Zapatistas continued to operate in Morelos, Michoacán, and Guerrero. In addition, hundreds of smaller bands were active throughout the country.[16]

Conditions were no better a year later. In early 1918 the estimated number of guerrillas, rebels, and bandits was two thousand Zapatistas in the south, two thousand Villistas in the north, one thousand Yaqui Indians in the northwest, and nineteen thousand others in various bands in the east. Aguascalientes was the only state where internal order prevailed.[17]

During 1919, the Zapatistas began to disintegrate following the killing of Zapata, and the Villistas also began to disperse. But Carranza's control over the countryside still remained limited. The National Association for the Protection of Human Rights in Mexico reported 317 major outbreaks of disorder in the 112-day period between April 10 and July 31, 1919. Of these, 272 were attributed to anti-Carrancistas, 15 to bandits, 15 to military and police lawlessness, and only 3 to clashes between competing political groups. During the period surveyed, thirty-one towns were raided and seventy-two trains were dynamited or robbed.[18]

Former *federales,* led by Felix Díaz, tried to take advantage of this breakdown of public order to stage a comeback. Thirty-six ex-generals of the Federal Army formed the National Re-organization Army of Mexico in Veracruz. Their October 1, 1918, revolutionary proclamation appealed not only to all former *federales* but also to all revolutionaries then in opposition to Carranza. The promised reward was restoration of the highest military rank previously held.[19]

Carranza's problems of internal order were partly of his own making. His insistence upon complete dissolution of the *federales* in 1914 eliminated an old organized army before a new army was prepared to assume order-keeping tasks. The military talents of some Federal officers might have been put to better use by Carranza—as they had by Villa and Zapata—in building a new national army.[20] Then, too, Carranza alienated many zealous revolutionaries by his failure to implement agrarian reform, by his suppression of organized labor (as in the Tampico oil strike of 1919), and by his apparent indifference to electoral fraud, such as Colonel Carlos S. Orozco's use of machine guns to make off with the ballot boxes in the Tampico election of 1919.[21]

It was quite unfair, however, to place all the blame on Carranza, as one newspaper did, "for the most scandalous tolerance for robberies committed by the high chiefs on a grand scale, for the most complete neglect of all efforts at organization, and for the utter inefficiency of the government in pacifying the country."[22] For the President was virtually powerless to restrain the victorious revolutionary generals. These were proud and ambitious men, revered by their troops and the local populace. Carranza either had to yield to their demands for local autonomy or face new defections. Eighteen out of thirty governorships were held by generals and colonels. Half of these were elected by the people; the other half simply shot their way into office.[23]

Mexico's politics had retrogressed to pre-Díaz conditions; the central government had lost control over the outlying states. When the Díaz system collapsed and the Federal Army was disbanded, the condition of the states changed from satrapies held in bondage to the central government by an officer loyal to the dictator into autonomous fiefs ruled by the local military commanders. The battalions and regiments of the various states were loyal only to the military governors or, if the governor was a civilian, to the Jefe de Operaciones Militares.[24]

During 1916, for example, the Governor of Sonora, General

Plutarco Elías Calles, simply ignored those orders from Carranza that happened to conflict with his own ideas; the Governor of Sinaloa, Angel Flores, issued his own paper money; and the Governor of Lower California, General Esteban Cantú, refused to turn over revenues collected in that state to the central government.[25] In 1917, the people of Puebla recognized no other authority than that of the military governor, who generally ignored Carranza's orders.[26] In Chihuahua, in 1918, General Francisco Murguía, the Chief of Military Operations, deposed Governor Ignacio C. Enríquez, whom Carranza had appointed, for alleged interference in military matters and selected his own man as governor.[27] And in Veracruz, in 1919, when the Supreme Court ordered a stay of execution for an ex-Federal officer, General Guadalupe Sánchez shot him anyway and was promoted shortly thereafter.[28]

Not only did the revolutionary generals assert their "right" to rule, but they ruled in a manner which was a **PREDATORY MILITARISM 1916 1919** credit neither to themselves, their institution, nor the Carranza government. More often than not they were predatory, venal, cruel, and corrupt. Thus, the new army leaders took on the worst characteristics of the Federal Army leaders they deposed.

But there was a difference. Militarism under Díaz was based upon a centralized system of hierarchy, organization, discipline and order, whereas under Carranza it was based upon audacity, improvisation, insubordination, and disorder. A contemporary Spanish observer, Vicente Blasco Ibañez, was shocked at the "scandalously young" generals. "Rustic illiterates," he called them, "mouthing liberty, democracy and other things they don't understand"; men who "maintain control of inferiors by a firing squad." He observed that they "become indignant if you accuse them of militarism; they all claim they are simple revolutionaries, that they want to be nothing more than citizens, but the fact is that they already form a separate caste which lives apart from the rest of the nation."[29]

Militarism probably was an inevitable by-product of the financial chaos, the unemployment, the precarious food supply, the bandit-guerrilla activity, and the popular disillusionment with the central government that characterized the years from 1916 to 1919. The lawyers, professors, engineers, and doctors who were better qualified to govern were prevented from doing so by men who knew nothing about law and whose only expertise was the art of violence.

Mexico's social cataclysm produced political conditions completely inimical to moral progress. When the rule of law, which both Madero and Carranza had tried to instill, was replaced by the use of force, the means began to corrupt the man, and revolutionary idealism soon succumbed to cynical opportunism.

Out of the revolutionary experience had grown up a new respect for force, and revolutionary chieftains were quick to appreciate the Machiavellian dictum that a commander should not mind being thought cruel, for the reputation for cruelty served the dual purpose of instilling fear in one's enemies and terror, mingled with respect, amongst one's troops. When the German consul pleaded in the name of humanity that the Constitutionalists spare the lives of Federal officers taken prisoner, Obregón replied that "the captured officers have already been executed, and this will continue to be done with all those who fall into our hands."[30] He was just as stern with fellow revolutionaries, for immediately following the battle of Celaya he executed 120 Villista officers.[31] Such battlefield practices by military men soon extended to civilian opponents. Villa set the tone when he occupied the capital in late 1914 and an orgy of assault and murder ensued. General Rudolfo Fierro simply assassinated those who had the audacity to criticize Villa.[32]

Under Carranza such practices remained common in the years from 1916 to 1919. Vengeful officers and unruly troops frequently assaulted civilians in Mexico City.[33] Carrancista Colonel Jesús M. Guajardo tricked Zapata into a meeting in 1919, then gunned him down, an exploit for which he was rewarded with fifty thousand pesos and promotion to brigadier general.[34]

Conditions in the states were equally bad. The so-called "preconstitutional" government of Oaxaca consisted of a general as governor, three colonels, and numerous lieutenants. Interested mainly in acquiring wealth, the military rulers practiced selective assassination to acquire property and exact tribute. They deliberately allowed widespread crime and banditry to go unpunished lest peace bring "constitutional" government, and with it an end to their racketeering and an accounting for their crimes.[35] In the oil fields around Tampico the populace much preferred the rule of bandit-guerrilla chieftain Manuel Pelaez to Carranza's Jefes de Operaciones Militares, a whole succession of whom had been brutal and corrupt.[36]

Through Carranza himself was personally honest, he had little choice but to permit the victorious generals to enrich themselves by graft, looting, and chicanery. And he had to go even further than that. He was obliged to bribe the officers corps to keep them loyal. *Divisionarios* got five thousand pesos "extra" per month; others were rewarded in conformity with rank. The *subtenientes*, the lowest ranking officers, received a thirty peso per month gratuity.[37]

In the time-honored Mexican tradition, troop commanders continued to pad the muster rolls. The treasury paid for feeding and supplying 100,000 men, although the actual numbers on the payroll were from 20 to 40 per cent less, and Carranza asked no questions lest he provoke a rebellion. Chief practitioner of the art of muster-roll padding was General Pablo González, the former flour-mill worker who became a millionaire by 1919,[38] as did an odd assortment of peddlers, ranchers, salesmen, photographers, mechanics, and school teachers who rose to the rank of general during the course of the Revolution. In the capital, reporter Ernest Gruening described their "flaunting of demimondaines, whom they loaded with diamonds, the acquisition of sumptuous mansions, the sporting of high-powered cars, [and] the trail of revelry from office to brothel."[39]

In the states, the military rulers often were too preoccupied with graft to be concerned over the bandit-guerrilla problem. In Chihuahua, for example, Villa was able to operate with impunity. In fact, some officers even sold Villa horses and ammunition. And the military guard on one of the trains in Chihuahua actually robbed the passengers.[40] In 1917, United States Consular Agent Parker reported from the Querétaro Constituent Convention that the greatest problem in the Carranza government was graft. The whole government, he observed, "rests upon a rotten foundation and, therefore, can endure no longer than the force of arms which placed it in power."[41] Two years later, the situation had not changed as military rulers and military bureaucrats continued to enrich themselves at public expense. In many communities, the officers were looked on as "the worst kind of robbers instead of protectors of the peace."[42]

THE MILITARY AND THE 1917 CONSTITUTION

Many revolutionaries were sincere idealists rather than cynical opportunists, and personal opportunism and revolutionary idealism were often found in the same person. Blasco Ibañez got the impression that nearly all the young revolutionary generals were socialists, many of them attempting "to imitate the bolsheviks."[43]

Once the Villistas had been beaten, the remaining generals closed ranks in support of Carranza for the first permanent presidency. On October 23, 1916, while plans were discussed for returning to a constitutional government, the top six *divisionarios* (Alvaro Obregón, Pablo González, Benjamin Hill, Francisco Coss, Cándido Aguilar, and Jesús Augustín Castro) pronounced him the *Primer Jefe*.[44] Shortly thereafter they organized the Liberal Constitutionalist Party to insure his election.

In view of the notorious failure of the military convention at Aguascalientes two years earlier, Carranza now assumed that he might successfully establish a civilian government. Accordingly, in the fall of 1916 he called for a popular election of delegates, *federales* and Villistas excluded, to write a new constitution, and of 221 delegates, only 45 military men were elected.[45] As the constituent convention opened at Querétaro in late 1916, Carranza presented the delegates with plans for constitutional reforms, all of them the products of studies undertaken by his civilian advisors.[46] These plans revealed that the *Primer Jefe* was interested in only moderate social reform and that, in accordance with his legalistic approach to the nation's problems, his main objective was to frame a new code of laws for Mexico. The military chieftains, however, were not in agreement with Carranza about the proposed character and philosophy of the new government. They were opposed to the President and his civilian advisors on two fundamental grounds. First of all, they had no intention of subordinating themselves to the civilians. Not only did they refuse to admit to any civilian superiority in the political realm, but they were also most reluctant to give up the officeholding opportunities they had won during the Revolution. Secondly, the military were more radical than Carranza, and thus more inclined toward social reforms than were the civilians at the convention.

Thus, the military delegates, under the influence of the *divisionario* lobbyists in the background, resisted the attempts of Carranza's civilian advisors, led by Felix Palavicini, to dominate the proceedings at Querétaro.[47] In reaction, Carranza's so-called *Renovador* group issued a bitter statement challenging the political competence of military men and demanding their subordination. In reply the military delegates demonstrated that they wielded a power over the constituent convention far in excess of their numbers, for they prohibited the newspapers from printing the statement.[48] In early January 1917, a United States government observer at the Querétaro Convention reported: "Practically all the oratorical talent in the present Congress is on the civil side but the voting power appears to be on the military side. It is curious that the civilian element is supporting Carranza's project which apparently is not sufficiently radical for the military. . . . It is generally believed that since the strength of the military element has been shown the work of the Congress will progress more or less peaceably."[49]

This dichotomy between civilian conservatives and military radicals is not entirely accurate, for both civilian and military camps were split into left, right, and moderate camps as follows:[50]

	left	*right*	*moderate*
civilian	78	81	71
military	33	11	1

However, it is true that civilians controlled the right while the military element, even though outnumbered by civilian intellectuals, labor leaders, and agrarians, who were of one mind on the issue of social reforms, dominated the left. The military delegates, headed by Generals Francisco Mújica and Heriberto Jara, were the real Jacobins of the convention. Most of them acted as though they were personal representatives of General Obregón. Their opinions were genuinely revolutionary; they were closer to the workers and peasants than Carranza, and they forced Carranza's civilian supporters to accept the revolutionary education, land reform, labor, and anticlerical articles of the new Constitution.[51]

Revolutionary writers have argued against the concept of a civilian-military dichotomy at Querétaro. They point out that there were no professional soldiers present, that Carranza himself was both a military leader and a civilian, and that the same was true of all forty-five uniformed delegates to the convention. These delegates—so the argument runs—defended the Revolution with words, not swords, at Querétaro; they were civilian amateurs, who had fought against the professional soldiers who had so long repressed the Mexican people.[52]

In opposition to this notion, it can be argued that civilian origins do not make revolutionary leaders less military minded than professional soldiers once a revolution triumphs. Díaz, for that matter, had originally been a civilian amateur. And Obregón, Villa, Calles, and other officers who were products of revolution not only maintained invidious distinctions between themselves and civilians in the immediate aftermath of victory, but these distinctions became even more pronounced with the passage of time.

Some writers have viewed the 1917 constitution as a civilian reaction against such military outrages as the assassination of Madero.[53] In support of this thesis they point to a number of clauses in the Constitution which strike at the political influence of the military. Article 82, for example, excludes from the presidency any person who in the past had figured directly, or indirectly, in an uprising, mutiny, or *cuartelazo* against the government. Yet support of this clause, especially support by the military delegates, is understandable mainly in terms of the desire of the revolutionary chieftains to bar forever, not only the *federales,* but also the Villistas and Zapatistas. A decade later, when the military men completely dominated Mexican politics, they deleted the original restriction in article 82 from the Constitution.[54]

Article 13 has also been interpreted as antimilitary. It had to do with the old *fuero militar,* which excluded the civil courts from trying military men even for civil crimes. The Ley Juárez of 1855 abolished these legal sanctuaries for the military and limited the jurisdiction of military courts to "crimes that had precise connection with military discipline only."[55] Article 13 of the 1917 constitution made no change, whatsoever, in the existing law. It read: "The military code exists for crimes and offenses against military discipline; but the military tribunals may in no case and for no cause extend their jurisdiction over persons who do not belong to the army. Should a civilian be implicated in a crime or offense of a military character, the proper civilian authorities shall hear the case."

What is often forgotten is that the civilians at Querétaro attempted to abolish all military courts, but in these efforts they were blocked by the military. General Mújica argued that military courts were necesary, not only to deal with problems of military justice but also with those involving discipline. Any civilian who feared persecution by military courts, he added, could avoid this simply by not volunteering for military service. Article 13 was approved 122 to 61.[56]

Other references to the military in the Constitution such as Articles 9 ("no armed assembly has the right of deliberating");

44

25 ("no member of the army may, in time of peace, be lodged in a private home without the consent of the owner"); 55, 58, and 81 (senators and deputies, to qualify for Congress, "may not be in active service for at least ninety days prior to the elections," and for the presidency, "six months"); and 129 ("no military authority may, in time of peace, engage in duties other than those that are directly connected with military affairs"), were routine clauses normally found in any modern constitution and were not even debated by the delegates. For these reasons it is difficult to accept the view that the 1917 Constitution was an antimilitary document.

By 1916 the Constitutional- **INCIPIENT** 1916
ist Army was swollen to over **PROFESSIONALISM** 1920
200,000 troops commanded by fifty thousand officers, over five hundred of whom claimed the rank of general. In the fight against Villa, just as in the struggles against Díaz and Huerta, local aspirants for military fame simply created their own armies and handed out grades and promotions at will. Since the revolutionary chieftains had recruited their armies from the local populace, they considered their troops as their personal property, and, as already noted, the troops in turn developed strong personal loyalties to the local *jefes*. Neither officers nor enlisted men were eager to perform services outside their home region, and they resisted integration into a larger national organization.[57]

In order to create a national army, Carranza had to break down these local loyalties. This task he assigned to War Minister Obregón early in 1916. Obregón succeeded in dissolving the major Constitutionalist armies of division strength—his own Army of the Northwest, González's Army of the East, Salvador Alvarado's Army of the Southeast, and Jacinto B. Treviño's Army of the Northeast—and in bringing most of the division generals under the direct command of the War Ministry.[58] He was far less successful in his attempts to integrate the scattered local forces into a national organization of ten divisions, seventy-five brigades, and two hundred fifty battalions. The problem here was not only to destroy local loyalties, but also to get rid of the excess officers. In mid-March, 1916, in an attempt to resolve both problems, Obregón declared a new order of battle for a reorganized national army, as follows:

	jefes (colonels)	*oficiales* (majors & lieutenants)	*tropas* (enlisted & non-coms)
artillery	133	966	5,890
cavalry	1,128	6,020	50,125
infantry	1,200	8,500	58,424
special services	177	2,066	11,384
totals	2,638	17,552	125,823

There were to be eleven *divisionarios,* fifty-five *generales de brigada,* and one hundred thirty-eight *brigadieres.*[59]

Since the table of organization called for only twenty thousand officers, thirty thousand of those who claimed officer rank in the Constitutionalist Army had to be retired. To induce them to do so voluntarily, Obregón established the Legion of Honor of the National Army. Any officer could join by withdrawing from active service, whereupon he would continue to keep his rank and receive his pay just as though he were in active service. Those excess officers who refused to retire voluntarily had their service records investigated by special Comisiones Revisoras de Hojas, which determined whether a man merited his presumed rank and whether he was excess. In the latter event, the officer in question was removed from active duty and assigned at full rank and half pay to the Depósito de Jefes y Oficiales. This meant he was placed in the Army Reserve and presumably was on call if his country needed him.[60]

The Carranza government received an avalanche of complaints, which were generally ignored, from those who felt they had been dealt with unjustly by the Comisiones Revisoras. The excess officers were quick to join the military uprising against Carranza in 1920. Excess enlisted men, like the officers, were placed in the First Reserve of the Army, but received no pay.

This also increased military hostility toward the President.

As the Revolution had destroyed the Colegio Militar and all other officer-training facilities, the army of 1916 was commanded by officers without professional knowledge. In the War Ministry, General Francisco Urquizo was appointed to head the Departamento del Estado Mayor (General Staff Department), and during the summer of 1916 he organized a General Staff system for all divisions. General Urquizo also established an Academia del Estado Mayor (General Staff Academy) to train officers for one hundred fifty new staff assignments. In the fall of 1916, Obregón inaugurated a new officer training school, and seventy young cadets from civilian life entered the first class. When the Colegio Militar was reopened on January 1, 1920, enrollment was 240.[61]

Obregón resigned as War Minister on May 1, 1917, the day Carranza became Constitutional President and the day the Ejército Constitucionalista formally changed its name to the Ejército Nacional.[62] Obregón had had his differences with Carranza both at the Convention of Aguascalientes in 1915 and at the Querétaro Convention in 1916-1917. For "reasons of health," he resigned his commission as division general, and returned to civilian pursuits in Sonora.

During the remainder of Carranza's term, the reorganization and development of the National Army continued. During 1917 the Departamento de Establecimientos Fabriles y Aprovisionamientos Militares was created to manufacture and repair war materials. In 1918, aviation and special services schools were organized, plus schools where recruits were taught to read and write.[63]

And yet, despite Carranza's efforts, when his term of office drew to a close, very little progress had been made toward building an effective national army. Blasco Ibañez thought it one of the most decrepit and inefficient military organizations he had ever seen—sloppily uniformed troops, grotesquely outfitted officers with big sombreros, enormous crossed cartridge belts, prominently displayed revolvers, excessive decorations, and a complete absence of professional training and knowledge. "Battles are won not by strategy," he observed, "but by who has the most ammunition," and, despite the heavy propaganda in behalf of ideals, he opined "the troops don't really know or care what they are fighting for." Another curiosity, he felt, was that this was "an army of two sexes," with *soldaderas* living alongside their men in the camps or, when on maneuvers, proceeding on ahead to prepare the meals.[64]

Local commanders, Jefes de Operaciones Militares, and military governors continued to ignore orders from either the President or the War Minister. The 1917 Constitution made matters worse by creating a National Guard, which was authorized to elect its own officers in each locality.[65] In addition, despite the substantial size of the army, special security forces had to be created to help maintain public order in Puebla, México, and various states in southern Mexico.[66] Muster rolls continued to be padded. There were 125,000 troops in the table of organization in 1918, but there were probably no more than fifty to sixty thousand in actual service. These had to deal with rebel and bandit forces numbering 25,000.[67]

Finally, Carranza made no progress whatsoever in reducing the enormous military drain upon the national budget. In 1914, when the Constitutional Army triumphed, the military budget amounted to 31 per cent of the total, but by 1917, the year Carranza became Constitutional President, it had risen to an all-time high of 72 per cent. It was still 66 per cent in 1919.[68] Such was the price President Carranza was obliged to pay for military support of his administration. But in the end it availed him nothing.

1920 AGUA PRIETA A presidential election in Mexico is always a time of political crisis. The one scheduled for July 1920 precipitated unusually early pre-election activity. The issue had already been posed in Querétaro in 1917. Were Carranza's civilian moderates or Obregón's military radicals going to govern Mexico? Although the military, with labor and peasant support, succeeded in writing their revolutionary philosophy into the 1917 Constitution, President Carranza did little to implement that constitution. He held up agrarian reform; the National Agrarian Commission redistributed less than one-half million acres during his entire term of office. He prevented urban labor from achieving the rights they had been guaranteed in the 1917 Constitution; he frequently called out troops to break strikes.

As a result, organized labor turned against Carranza. They had joined him in the struggle against Villa, contributing the famous, but not very effective, six Red Battalions of fighting workers. This they had done in exchange for Carranza's January 1915 guarantees of social and economic advances for labor. But

as provisional president, Carranza forgot his promises. In late 1915 and again early in 1916, he ordered striking labor leaders tried in the military courts; War Minister Obregón, however, acquitted them all.[69] Repeatedly frustrated, despite their victory at Querétaro in 1917, the labor leaders organized in the summer of 1918 the Confederación Regional Obrera Mexicana (CROM); inside it they set up a political action group to promote Obregón for the presidency.

Carranza objected to such politicking a full two years before his term expired. A January 15, 1919, executive proclamation ordered a moratorium on politics till the end of the year so that the Revolution might be consolidated.[70] But by spring the press was already speculating about likely presidential candidates, and the only prominent *"presidenciables"* mentioned were all *divisionarios*—Obregón, González, Alvarado, and Diéguez.[71] Obviously, the popular expectation was that the military would take over the executive branch of government in 1920.

The President's main worry was the ambitious and powerful Obregón. In an attempt to reduce his military strength in Sonora, in May 1919, Carranza called Governor Calles to Mexico City to become Minister of Industry and Communications, appointed Governor-elect Aldolfo de la Huerta Consul General in New York City, ordered the transfer from Sonora of Obregonista Generals Roberto Cruz and Francisco Serrano, and arranged for Carrancista General Ignacio Pesqueira to assume the governorship of Sonora.[72]

Obregón, who till then felt that Carranza ultimately would be forced to designate him heir apparent, was impelled to action by these events. In early June, he publicly criticized Carranza, declared his own candidacy, and pledged that if elected president he would clean up the widespread corruption in the government.[73] The President countered by announcing his support for his civilian ambassador to Washington, Ignacio Bonillas. The President was surprised and shaken by the announcement of the candidacy of General Pablo González, the head of the Carrancista military faction.[74] Consequently, as soon as the

50

campaign formally got underway in November 1919, Carranza began reemphasizing his civilian thesis of government, condemning militarism and praetorianism, and calling for the election of another nonmilitary president like himself. Carranza argued "we should not elect a military man but a civilian, and he must be a man of culture, of ample preparation, able to resolve the great diplomatic problems with which we shall be faced."[75] Carranza's son-in-law, General Cándido Aguilar, then Governor of Veracruz, chimed in with a call for the elimination of all military governors and military politicians.[76]

The Obregonists objected violently to the epithet of militarism. They emphasized Obregón's civilian qualifications for president and the fact that he was not a professional soldier. After each glorious military service to the nation, they maintained, he had resigned from the army and returned to civilian life. In a memorial to the Senate on September 12, 1919, Obregón stated that he no longer wanted to be considered a member of the National Army, and he requested that his commission be taken away since he lacked the vocational desire for a career in arms. "My spirit is *civilista*," he contended, "for three times in my life [that is, against Orozco, Huerta, and Villa] I have had to combat the excesses of militarism in our country." He explained, almost apologetically, that only when the liberty and unity of the nation were threatened by militarism did he resort to the necessary use of force in order to destroy it.[77] Similarly, General Pablo González and his supporters repeatedly denied during the campaign that they were in any sense militarists.

This *civilismo-militarismo* issue during the period from 1919 to 1920 has been the object of much conflicting interpretation. General Barragán sees Obregón's drive for the presidency as pure militaristic *"futurismo."* He finds Obregón jealous of General González's popularity, and charges him with an unscrupulous use of force, including connivance with ex-Federal officers in order to attain the presidency.[78] Similarly, General Rubén García views the Agua Prieta uprising of April 1920, as a *"nefarious cuartelazo"* carried out by politically ambitious generals who, just like the men who ousted Madero, had little scruple about assassinating the President in order to attain their ends.[79] And Hector de la Rosa contrasts "loyal and responsible" Carrancista Generals Diéguez, Murguía, and Lucio Blanco with "ambitious militarists" such as Obregón and González.[80]

Defenders of Obregón see the matter quite differently. González Ramírez argues that Carranza, who assumed the title Primer Jefe del Ejército Constitucionalista for so long, was just as much a military man as Obregón, that *"civilismo"* in behalf of the Carranza "puppet" Bonillas was simply electoral propaganda put forth by the Carrancista military faction, the self-enriched part of the army.[81] And it is true that those generals who campaigned for Bonillas were motivated by the personal advantages they enjoyed as political agents of the Carranza regime.[82]

Blasco Ibañez also viewed the *civilismo-militarismo* issue as an artificial one. Such campaign posters as

"BONILLAS REPRESENTS THE DEATH OF MILITARISM"

and

"IF YOU WISH TO END REVOLUTIONS, VOTE FOR BONILLAS,"

he derided by pointing out that some of the most notorious militarists were backing Bonillas. He ridiculed as "great lies" the declarations of Obregón and González that they were simple citizens who had abandoned their arms. He observed that despite the fact that the Mexican people were tired of violence and revolution "200,000 Mexicans sustain themselves by militarism."[83]

In fact, the army was campaigning on three fronts, for Bonillas, Obregón, and González each had a substantial military following. But the bulk of the armed forces gave their support to General Obregón, and this was crucial in blocking Bonillas. Carranza might have had a better chance of imposing a civilian successor if he had chosen a civilian, such as Luis Cabrera, who at least had figured prominently in the Revolution.[84] But to select a political unknown, whom Obregón could ridicule as a "magnificent bookkeeper," was obviously a mistake. It was sim-

52

ply too much to expect that military men, convinced the army had made the Revolution, would accept the management of their handiwork by someone not authentically a revolutionary. In a sense, Carranza's problem was chronological. He was attempting to introduce civilian rule at a time in the revolutionary cycle when the military were still politically dominant.

Once the issue had been drawn, only violence could resolve it. Obregón, implying that the government clearly intended to rig the elections, promised the army he would "recover liberty and return it to the people." He concluded a secret pact with labor promising various privileges, favors, and rights in exchange for its backing.[85] Meanwhile, Carranza began replacing all known Obregónistas in the army and in the bureaucracy. Some, such as Calles, resigned of their own volition in early 1920. In March, Obregón charged that all his military supporters were being persecuted while those supporting Bonillas were given every protection.[86] Carranza's response was to name Obregón's rival, General Diéguez, Minister of War. Obregón, on campaign, thereupon began private talks with key military men, such as General Arnulfo Gómez in the Tampico petroleum region, about a possible course of violent action. Carranza attempted to ward this off by summoning Obregón to the capital for questioning in connection with General Robert F. Cejudo's treason trial, and by ordering General Ignacio Pesqueira to take over as Governor of Sonora from Adolfo de la Huerta.[87]

The upshot of all the foregoing was the April 23, 1920 Plan of Agua Prieta, issued in defense of both Obregón and de la Huerta by the Sonora military leaders—Generals Calles, Angel Flores, Francisco R. Manzo, Roberto Cruz, Francisco R. Serrano, and Alejandro Monge, and Colonels Abelardo Rodríguez, J. M. Aguirre, and Fausto Topete. These men created the Ejército Liberal Constitucionalista (Liberal Constitutionalist Army), designating Governor de la Huerta *Jefe Supremo,* in order to defend the sovereignty of Sonora. Carranza, they charged, was attempting *"imposición"* of a president objectionable to the Mexican people.[88]

53

Obregón, who had escaped from Mexico City, rushed back to head the movement. Within a few days he was marching down the west coast at the head of an army of rebel Sonorans and Yaqui Indians. By the end of April allegiance had been given to the Plan of Agua Prieta by the principal military commanders in the east (Generals Arnulfo Gómez in Tampico and Lázaro Cárdenas in Veracruz), in the north (Generals Francisco Urbalejo, Ignacio Enríquez, Eugenio Martínez, J. Gonzalo Escobar, and Joaquín Amaro in Chihuahua), and in the west (Generals Fortunato Maycotte in Guerrero, Alberto Pineda in Michoacán, and Carlos Greene in Tabasco). As Obregón's swelling army approached the capital, General Pascual Ortiz Rubio joined him with Michoacán troops, and Obregón's righthand man from Sonora, General Benjamín Hill, then in charge of the troops in the Federal District, turned against the Carranza government. When it was apparent that Obregón would prevail, Generals Pablo González and Jacinto B. Treviño, long close to Carranza and indebted to him for nearly all their military honors and opportunities, also joined the rebel movement. Of the prominent revolutionary generals, only Manuel Diéguez in Jalisco, Cesario Castro in Torreón, Cándido Aguilar in Veracruz, and Francisco Murguía, Francisco Urquizo, and Juan Barragán in the Federal District, remained loyal to their old *Primer Jefe*. On the 14th of May, Carranza's pathetic little column, supported only by the cadets of the Colegio Militar and the troops of the few loyal generals, abandoned Mexico City and fled eastward. A week later, after his army had virtually dissolved, Carranza was shot in his sleep by General Rudolfo Herrero.[89]

On the issues of whether Carranza was acting in violation of the law and the Constitution in trying to impose Bonillas as his successor, and of whether the army had the right to make a political judgment with respect to the issue of *imposición,* the partisans of Carranza or Obregón will never agree. The important consideration, however, is that the army did assert its political power by the use of force. The radical young generals, most of them still in their twenties and thirties, decided the time had come to depose their seventy-year-old *Primer Jefe*. To them, Carranza was out of step with popular opinion and had turned his back upon the revolutionary principles for which they had fought.

And it cannot be denied that, in 1920, Obregón was the popular, as well as the military, choice for president, for he was backed by both the urban and rural masses, whereas Carranza enjoyed only middle- and upper-class support. General González was supported by clergymen, *hacendados*, and foreign investors—the same groups which had backed Porfirio Díaz.[90]

What did the Agua Prieta rebellion mean in terms of Mexico's social Revolution? It meant that the moderate phase had come to an end and that the radicals were now assuming power. Briefly united, the moderates and radicals had destroyed the conservatives in 1914, but after that they soon began to fight each other. The Villa-Carranza struggle of 1915 may be viewed as the first attempt of the radicals to take power. It failed, but only temporarily, and in the Obregón triumph of 1920 the process was completed.[91] Under the aegis of the Sonoran caudillos the Jacobin phase of the Mexican revolution was about to begin.

1920-1924

III

THE OBREGON ERA

OBREGÓN AND HIS GOVERNMENT

When General Alvaro Obregón marched into Mexico City in the spring of 1920 at the head of a rebel army of forty thousand, it marked the sixth time in nine years that the central government had been overturned by force. Largely because of the political reforms of Obregón, this never occurred again. He was the first to visualize and to implement successfully an entirely new set of control techniques. These essentially involved a broadening of the base of support for the central government. Obregón achieved this by curbing the local military chieftains and by developing labor and peasant counterpoises to the military. By playing various power groups off against one another, Obregón greatly enhanced the strength of the central government in general, and that of the president in particular.

57

Obregón, the first general of the Revolution to serve as President of Mexico, was white, like Madero and Carranza, but unlike them he was no aristocrat. His parents had been poor Spanish immigrants. Alvaro, born in Sonora in 1880 and the youngest of eighteen children, improved his station in life by taking advantage of the new economic opportunities available under the Díaz prosperity. His sisters taught him to read and write; in his teens he became a blacksmith; in his early twenties he successively managed a small flour mill, a mechanics shop, and served as agent for a farm machinery concern. In 1904, he rented some farmland, grew and marketed chickpeas on it, invented a machine for sowing chickpeas, and began to purchase land. By 1910, with his five hundred acres, he was considered a successful middle-class farmer.[1]

Up to age thirty, Alvaro Obregón was so preoccupied with domestic problems—he married in 1902, but his wife died in 1907, leaving him with two small children—and small business problems, that he had little time, or concern, for politics. Madero's revolutionary triumph changed all that. Encouraged by friends, and with Maderista support, he won the presidency of the municipal council of Huatabampo, Sonora, in late 1911. In the spring of 1912, when the Orozquista rebellion threatened Sonora, Governor José María Maytorena called on all municipal presidents for emergency help in defending the state. Obregón recruited three hundred men, most of them small farmers, and was commissioned a lieutenant colonel of the Sonora irregulars.[2]

It was this military experience which transformed the man and gave rise to his boundless ambition. For in the field he displayed the most natural talent for soldiering. Following the defeat of Orozco, Obregón had returned only a few months to civilian life when he felt obliged to take up arms against Huerta, and his brilliant organizational and fighting abilities soon gained him command of the Constitutionalist Army of the Northwest. This invincible general—he never lost a battle —was soon the most feared and respected soldier in Mexico.

Under Carranza, it was he who administered the surrender of the Federal Army; it was he who stopped Villa from taking control of the Revolution, and it was he who began to build the new National Army. But once Carranza became Constitutional president in 1917, the hitherto close relationship between the general and the President began to cool. As already indicated, not only was Carranza apprehensive of the ambitions of his popular and powerful War Minister, but he also considered Obregón too radical politically. Obregón's retirement to civilian life in 1917 only postponed the inevitable clash between these two powerful revolutionary personalities.

Obregón had long been worried about militarism. As early as 1915 he had warned Carranza that the treason, brutality, corruption, and personal opportunism of the revolutionary leaders was damaging the good name of the Constitutionalist Army.[3] And understandably he was most upset, after resigning as War Minister, to see so little implementation of his program of military reforms. Because of the ineffectiveness of Carranza in military matters, the army became demoralized and defected to Obregón in 1920.

Once in power, Obregón was determined to make drastic changes in armed forces organization. But before going too far, too fast, he first had to secure broader popular support in order to protect himself against the opposition from the *generales* and *jefes* that his military reforms would provoke.

Obregón became aware of the power potential of urban labor as early as 1915 when the Casa de Obrera Mundial supplied him with six battalions of workers in the fight against Villa. And both at the 1917 constitutional convention and during the 1919-1920 presidential campaign, the workers' support of the military position had contributed to the defeats of Carranza.

Following the 1920 rebellion, labor was amply rewarded. CROM leader Luis Morones was put in charge of the military factories and General Celestino Gasca, the labor leader who had commanded the workers' battalions, was made Governor of the Federal District. The guarantees in the 1917 Constitution concerning the right to organize, the right to strike, minimum wages and maximum hours, were made a reality. In return, the Labor Party provided Obregón with his principal support in Congress, and organized labor formed a workers' militia to defend his administration.

This arrangement, however, became unsatisfactory to the President when the labor leaders became just as corrupt and brutal as the military chieftains. The CROM used strong-arm tactics against rival unions, blackmailed employers, called wildcat strikes, and even assassinated opposition Senator Francisco Field Jurado. To curb such violence and irresponsibility, Obregón used troops against labor during 1922 and 1923. As these crackdowns cooled labor's ardor for the President, Obregón turned to the peasants for support.[4]

To this end he began to redistribute agricultural holdings. Although for practical economic reasons the pace of agrarian reform was slower than agrarian leaders such as Antonio Díaz Soto y Gama would have liked, Obregón redistributed 2,500,000 acres, or nine times as much as Carranza.[5] The President's energetic new program to promote rural education also was designed to benefit the peons.

In courting labor and agrarian support, Obregón was simply acknowledging the growing power of new interest groups which had emerged from the turmoil of the Revolution. Already under Carranza's regime, though civilian bureaucrats ruled in the capital and military chieftains in the states, farm and union leaders began to organize their followers and to exert political pressures. The price Carranza and his military governors had to pay for their failure to accommodate these new interest groups was overwhelming peasant and worker support for Obregón's candidacy and for the rebellion he led in 1920. Then, under Obregón's presidency, both groups built up strong parties, organized voting blocs in Congress and began to exert their political weight.[6] These were the first important steps toward popular participation in politics.

This development of mass support was a key feature of Obregón's plan to establish a strong national government. The last such government had existed under Díaz, when the church, the business interests, and the landholders combined with the army to maintain effective sway at the center. The Madero revolution had broken the Díaz system, but neither Madero, nor Huerta, nor Carranza, could reestablish an effective new order. In place of the traditionalist forces, Obregón substituted workers and peasants as his civilian base, but like Díaz, he had to develop a disciplined and loyal army to establish a viable central government.

The immediate military tasks following Agua Prieta were to purge the army of all Carrancistas and to break the resistance of all generals unwilling to accept the hegemony of the Sonora clique then ensconced in Mexico City. These efforts began during the May-December 1920 interim presidency of Adolfo de la Huerta and took nearly two and one-half years to complete. The most pressing problem was General Pablo González. Although he had turned against Carranza, he also wanted to be president, and he had entered Mexico City with his army of twenty thousand ahead of Obregón in early May 1920. The issue was temporarily resolved by a simple show of force when the Obregonista armies commanded by Generals Benjamín Hill from Sonora, Fortunato Maycotte from Oaxaca, and Pascual Ortíz Rubio from Michoacán, began arriving in the capital. When their combined strength reached 25,000, General González felt obliged to withdraw northward to his home state of Nuevo León. In July Obregonista officers there arrested General González, claiming to have nipped in the bud a major military conspiracy. He was tried by a military court and condemned to die before a firing squad, but President de la Huerta pardoned him. Thereupon González fled to the United States where he continued to conspire. Meanwhile, de

THE MILITARY PROBLEM

la Huerta spent eight million of the eleven million pesos in the national treasury to purchase the loyalty of the Gonzalista military.[7]

Most Carrancista generals were dealt with summarily. Cándido Aguilar in Veracruz had fled into exile; Manuel Diéguez in Guadalajara and Francisco Murguía in Chihuahua were arrested and cashiered from the army; Jesús Guajardo was captured and shot. De la Huerta replaced all the Carrancista military governors and Jefes de Operaciones with Obregonistas. By December 1, 1920, when Obregón assumed the presidency following his overwhelming election victory in September, all the Carrancista generals had been removed from the army.[8]

De la Huerta also attempted, during his six months' provisional presidency, to pacify other military factions. The former *federales* were disappointed about pensions and employment opportunities. To General Félix Díaz, their self-appointed leader, de la Huerta paid fifty thousand pesos toward expenses of a trip abroad, but Díaz used the money to continue his plotting against the government.[9]

More successful were de la Huerta's negotiations with Pancho Villa. The bandit chieftain of the north agreed to incorporate all but fifty of his seven hundred men into the National Army and to become a law-abiding citizen provided the government would purchase for him the 200,000-acre hacienda of Canutillo on the border between Chihuahua and Durango. The price paid by de la Huerta was 800,200 pesos.[10] Although Obregón objected to these liberal arrangements, he too, as President, went to extraordinary lengths to keep Villa pacified. The more important items demanded by, and received by, Villa from Obregón during 1921, 1922, and 1923 included 10,000 pesos for uniforms for Villa's cavalrymen, 40,000 pesos for damages allegedly suffered to Villa's house in Ciudad Juárez, 50,000 pesos for Villa's check in that amount drawn on the Bank of London in 1913, 100,000 pesos for the purchase of agricultural equipment, and 5,000 pesos per month for pensions for "orphans, widows, and invalids at Canutillo."[11] These peace payments did not come to an end till Villa was assassinated by a group of local citizens on July 20, 1923.[12]

During the first two years of his presidency Obregón was challenged by assorted Felicista, Villista, Carrancista, and Gonzalista conspiracies. These were handled with brutal efficiency by his brilliant young War Minister, General Francisco R. Serrano, and by the latter's assistant, General Roberto Cruz. In June 1921, Gonzalista General Fernando Viscaino was charged with conspiracy and summarily shot. In February 1922, Brigadier General Antonio Pruneda in Coahuila was charged one afternoon with conniving with General Francisco Murguía; the next morning, following a hasty summary court martial in which his guilt was by no means proven, he was shot. A day later the same thing happened to Gonzalista General Antonio Ruiz in Chihuahua. In March 1922, seven colonels and majors in Durango were executed for "intention to rebel." In July 1922, two prominent Carrancistas, General Lucio Blanco and

63

Colonel Cándido Martínez, were kidnapped in Laredo and drowned in the Rio Grande.[13]

The most serious challenge came during the summer of 1922 from a combined movement of Carrancista generals headed by Francisco Murguía. The latter had been plotting in exile ever since Obregón released him in early 1921. His principal associates were Generals Juan Carrasco in the west, Carlos Greene in Yucatán, Cándido Aguilar and Miguel Alemán in the east, Domingo Arrieta and José V. Elizondo in the north, and Juan Urquiza in the south. But before their scheduled uprising could take place, Serrano's troops surprised and crushed the northern and western rebels and shot Murguía and Carrasco. Thereupon, the eastern and southern movements also collapsed.[14]

Although Obregón was generally free of troubles from the Carrancistas, Gonzalistas, Villistas and *federales* by the end of 1922, he was a long way from disciplining his own followers. There was still no national army. The Agua Prieta rebellion created a whole new collection of independent military chieftains, few of whom hesitated to take advantage, in the name of the Revolution, of opportunities for self-enrichment.

Obregón preferred more idealism and less opportunism in his colleagues, but he had to be practical and face up to the realities of dispersed power. To use force to curb the autonomy of the local military chieftains would be to provoke rebellions. Accordingly, Obregón adopted tactics similar to those used by Porfirio Díaz; that is, he encouraged the generals to exchange their political independence for material gain.

One of his major moves toward this end was to incorporate all persons claiming the rank of general (except Gonzalistas, Villistas, and Carrancistas) into the regular army. Obregón declared that "if a man says he is a general then he must be one," and would also be entitled to a general's pay and privileges.[15] His famous observation that "there is no general able to resist a *cañonazo* (cannon ball) of fifty thousand pesos" reflected his cynical conviction that loyalty often had to be purchased. One *cañonazo* for War Minister Serrano cost eighty thousand pesos.

That was the sum he lost gambling in a single night, and when he presented an expense voucher for this amount, Obregón ordered it paid.[16] Obregón fully appreciated the fact that most men joined the 1920 rebellion in order to gain something. To critics, he maintained that the only reason the thieving generals allowed him to become president was because he had only one arm—the other had been lost in the Battle of Ceyaya—and, therefore, he would be able to steal less.

The demands of Serrano were only the most notorious. Two examples from hundreds of a pettier variety were General Manuel J. Contreras' claim of five thousand pesos for "private expenses" incurred in the Agua Prieta uprising and General Rubén Culebra's request for 7500 pesos monthly as compensation for properties he lost fighting in behalf of the Revolution between 1914 and 1917.[17]

The most troublesome grafters were the Jefes de Operaciones who commanded the various military zones. Not content with their customary 10 per cent commission on all supplies and equipment purchased, they exacted loans from the local banks, sold gambling concessions, and blocked agrarian reforms or broke labor strikes in exchange for bribes from *hacendados* and employers. Obregón's desk was filled with complaints concerning the venality and brutality of the Jefes de Operaciones, coupled with pleas for their removal. In December 1921, the scandalous conduct of General Barajas in Jalisco was the subject of a congressional investigation.[18] In April 1922, officers in the Veracruz region were charged with abusing their privileges and violating the local women.[19] In the same month a telegram from the citizens of Tecali, Puebla, condemned two Obregonista generals as "villainous assassins."[20] In October 1922, the Chiapas Jefe de Operaciones, General Manuel Mendoza, forced a local bank to lend him thirty thousand pesos.[21] Chiapas Governor Amadeo Ruiz wrote Obregón the following month that the new Jefe de Operaciones, General Vicente González, was "insulting the citizenry, intervening in local politics, disarming the police," and, in general, stirring up an otherwise peaceful state.[22] In the spring of 1923 the workers and *campesinos* of Jalapa urged Obregón to remove as Jefe de Operaciones General Guadalupe Sánchez "because of his insults, crimes, and oppressions against the proletariat."[23]

The first two years of Obregón's rule were rife with bandit and rebel activity. As under Carranza, the local military chieftains were often so preoccupied with illegitimate activities that they neglected to perform their legitimate function of preserving internal order. During the summer of 1922, for example, the Yaqui Indians of Sonora frequently assaulted and robbed the Chinese merchants; the military in Zacatecas refused to help the farmers pursue the bandits; the military in Chihuahua failed to prevent bandit assaults on the passenger trains; and rebel bands operated with impunity in Tabasco.[24] On August 4, 1922, the United States Embassy reported assaults by bandits and rebels in the states Tamaulipas, Jalisco, Nuevo León, Guerrero, Oaxaca, Coahuila, Hidalgo, Durango, Sinaloa, Tabasco, and Puebla.[25]

The breakdown of law and order prompted most states to form citizens vigilante organizations. These were variously called *guardias blancas, defensas sociales,* and *cuerpos de voluntarios.* Such groups frequently clashed with the regulars who complained that civilians were interfering with their functions and should be disarmed. The vigilantes maintained they were acting legally under article 10 of the constitution, which guaranteed the "right to bear arms" to defend one's interests.[26] By 1923 the vigilantes were often as venal and brutal as the regulars, and, hence, Obregón ordered the army to confiscate their arms.[27]

There were also serious conflicts between the governors, backed by the state militias, and the Jefes de Operaciones. During 1922 the military and political authorities were at odds in nearly every state.[28] The most notorious rivalry was in Michoacán, where the governor, General Francisco Mújica, vied for supremacy with Generals Pascual Ortíz Rubio and Lázaro Cárdenas, but equally as serious were the troubles between the civilian governors and the Jefes de Operaciones in Coahuila, Zacatecas, Colima, Tamaulipas, Querétaro, and Guerrero.[29]

Even though thousands of Car- **BUILDING A** rancistas had been ousted, the **NATIONAL ARMY** army still numbered over 100,- 000 when Obregón became president. In response to the growing popular clamor that such a large and expensive military establishment was no longer necessary, Obregón promised to reduce it to fifty thousand.[30] To this end Obregón had Congress pass the Law of the First Reserve. It provided for incorporation of 452 generals, 2,290 colonels, and 8,318 junior officers into the reserve and for discharge of all the enlisted men under their commands. First Reserve officers, though retired from active service, drew half pay for two years and were allowed to retain their rank and to wear the uniform indefinitely.[31]

Obregón ordered his Jefes de Operaciones to compile the names of officers who might be made reservists. These lists were then carefully examined by the War Department's Comisiones Revisoras de Hojas for a final decision. Within nine months more than a thousand officers were declared "excess," and thereafter about fifty per month were retired.[32] As anticipated, the War Ministry was flooded with complaints from officers who charged they were being removed from the service without sufficient reason. In some cases, such as when General Saturnino Cedillo of San Luis Potosí and his large personal army objected, the government rescinded the retirement orders, but for the most part, War Minister Serrano ignored the complaints.[33]

To assist the officers and men in their return to civilian pursuits, Obregón set up military-agricultural colonies. Under the law, a discharged officer or soldier was permitted to purchase from the government a parcel of land, the size being dependent upon rank and grade, and to pay for it over a period of twenty years at 4 per cent interest.[34] Reliable statistics are not available, but indications are that few chose to join the agricultural colonies.

Within one year, Obregón reduced the army by thirty thousand; within two years by another ten thousand.[35] The effect was to drastically reduce military expenditures. Whereas the army absorbed 61 per cent of the total budget in 1921, Obregón's first year in the presidency, it took only 36 per cent in 1923 and 1924.[36]

While cutting down the army, Obregón made simultaneous efforts to bring it under control.[37] Determined to break down regional autonomy and the predatory militarism that accompanied it, he made it clear that officers' careers henceforth would depend upon their loyalty to the Ejército Nacional and the central government rather than to the local *jefes* and the states. In the spring of 1921 War Minister Serrano issued the following new table of organization:[38]

generals		318
division	18	
of brigade	72	
brigadiers	228	
jefes		3370
colonels	840	
lt. colonels	1014	
majors	1526	
oficiales		10,771
captains I	2429	
captains II	2021	
lieutenants	3265	
sub-lieutenants	3056	
troops		68,320
TOTAL		82,779
horses		36,482

At the same time the battalion and regimental structure was reorganized. As the large number of horses suggests, the cavalry became the largest branch of the army.[39] This reflected both the prominent role that mounted soldiers played in winning the

Revolution and the peculiar postrevolutionary requirements for maintaining internal order. Also, the general staff was enlarged and the already insignificant navy declined further. The changes are best illustrated by comparing the War Ministry budgets under Díaz and Obregón as follows:[40]

MINISTRY BUDGET

	fiscal 1907	fiscal 1921
secretary	3%	1%
general staff	3%	12%
infantry	28%	34%
cavalry	16%	35%
artillery	6%	6%
engineers	5%	3%
medical corps	3%	3%
navy	6%	3%
shops	12%	
other	18%	3%

In early 1923, Obregón increased the number of military districts from twenty to thirty-five, the ostensible reason being, now that rebel and bandit attacks were under control, large troop concentrations were no longer necessary.[41] But the real reason for so doing was to fragment further the regional military commands and thus reduce the danger of a challenge to the central government.

Obregón's efforts to render the army nonpolitical were complicated by the fact that the Agua Prieta movement was as much political as it was military. When that rebellion began, there had been seven division generals. Diéguez, Murguía, and Cesario Castro remained loyal to Carranza; Obregón, Jacinto B. Treviño, and Jesús Augustín Castro joined the rebellion; and Pablo González tried to use the opportunity to win power for himself. During the rebellion, the three Carrancistas and González were eliminated, but *divisionario* rank was bestowed upon Generals of Brigade Eulalio Gutiérrez, Francisco Cosío Robelo, Joaquín Amaro, Enrique Estrada, Fortunato Maycotte, Guada-

lupe Sánchez, Eugenio Martínez, Plutarco Elías Calles, and Francisco Coss as a reward for service rendered and to insure loyalty to the new government. Obregón hoped—in vain, for the most part—that these nine new *divisionarios* would find satisfactory nonpolitical career opportunities in the reorganized National Army.[42]

The President was sparing in his appointment of military men to public office. War Minister Serrano, Agriculture Minister Antonio Villarreal, and Interior Minister Calles were the only three in the cabinet, and there were only nine military governors—half as many as under Carranza—in the thirty-two states and federal territories.[43] Most of the military governors were the leading politicians in their respective states at the time of Obregón's inauguration, but from 1922 onward the President began to undermine them and to replace them with civilian appointees loyal to the central government.[44]

Obregón made repeated efforts, most of them futile, to restrict officers to the performance of military functions. He ordered all military commanders to abstain from talking to opposition politicians.[45] Defectors were cashiered from the army, and he confiscated their property.[46] During 1923, Obregón even began to discourage military support in behalf of official candidates. He issued a circular insisting that the army abstain from all political activity in the 1924 elections, for he did not want it to appear he was attempting to impose his successor.[47] The generals, however gained that impression anyway, and this was a major cause of the December 1923 rebellion.

Professionalism was an integral part of Obregón's program to reduce the political activity of the army. In a way, the President was carrying on where he left off in 1917 when he resigned as War Minister. By 1921, the Colegio Militar in Chapultepec had overhauled its whole instruction program. New courses and more competent instructors were introduced in the infantry and artillery departments, and a medical school and new departments of cavalry instruction and of aviation were created.[48] Inside the War Ministry, the General Staff, headed by Brigadier General Calixto Ramírez Garrido, organized a modern supply system and revised antiquated military laws.[49] Obregón, aware of Mexico's professional backwardness, dispatched a number of promising young officers to Spain, France, Germany, and the United States to study modern military techniques.[50]

Obregón's program of professionalism included enlisted men too. Primary instruction for all new army recruits was made

71

obligatory. Regulation uniforms were provided, and the men were obliged to wear them at all times.[51] Thus ended a decade of disdain by revolutionary soldiers for military garb. Henceforth, regulation uniforms were considered acceptable and were worn with pride. Finally, Obregón put the army to work. His dual aims in doing so were to keep it out of political mischief and to provide it with an economically productive function. In 1921, he created nineteen special work battalions for roadbuilding, irrigation development, and railroad and telegraph repair.[52]

THE 1923 REBELLION Obregón must have felt that all his efforts to build a nonpolitical, professional army had been in vain, for in December of 1923 he was faced with an army uprising which nearly toppled his government. Pro-Obregón writers have generally seen irresponsible militarism as the principal cause of the 1923 rebellion. "It represented an attempt to elevate the power of militarism," declared Manuel González Ramírez.[53] "It was a movement initiated by disloyal military men," wrote Obregón's biographer, Roberto Quiros Martínez.[54] "Caudillism," was the cause, said Emilio Portes Gil; "the trouble was that numerous division generals, as a result of Agua Prieta, had acquired prestige and now considered themselves factors in national politics."[55]

Clearly the rebel generals possessed warriors' mentalities. Because they made the Revolution, they felt entitled to political power. They were unwilling to confine themselves to a police-type role of defending the central government, particularly if it were not one of their own choosing[56]; they considered Obregón's attempt to control them as infringement upon their hard-earned regional prerogatives. They felt that the President was overly sympathetic to agrarian complaints about local military irresponsibility and that he often dismissed officers and transferred whole contingents of troops without sufficient cause. Also, Obregón's scheme to discharge over one thousand officers from the First Reserve made many reservists quite ready to join any

72

uprising which, if successful, might return them to active service and restore their military pay.[57]

Although the December 1923 uprising was primarily military, important civilian elements were also involved. A substantial segment of organized labor had become disenchanted with the government, particularly with the leadership of Luís Morones and General Celestino Gasca. Although the General Confederation of Workers and the railroad unions did not break with Obregón, many of their members fought for the rebels.[58] Then too, the administration's coalition of revolutionary political groups began to fragment, with those elements losing favor with the government seeking refuge by joining the rebellion. For example, the middle-class labor party, Partido Liberal Constitucionalista, which had spearheaded Obregón's election in 1920, lost out to a new official coalition party dominated by agrarian elements in the 1922 congressional elections.[59] Yet, during 1923, as the President's land reform policies were considered insufficiently aggressive, and as he began to disarm agrarian vigilante groups, a portion of his rural support began to wither away too.[60]

Obregón himself was largely responsible for the political crisis which precipitated the December 1923 rebellion. And the parallel between the 1920 and 1923 rebellions is indeed striking. The issue again was the presidential succession, and the armed struggle that ensued was again a result of the president's attempts to impose a successor unacceptable to certain military leaders. However, in contrast to 1920, *imposición* succeeded in 1923.

It was already clear by late 1922 that Obregón had chosen General Calles to succeed him for the 1924-1928 presidential term. But several other *divisionarios*, all in command of large bodies of troops, such as Guadalupe Sánchez in the east, Enrique Estrada in the west, and Fortunato Maycotte in the south, outranked Calles, and, accordingly, considered themselves more deserving of the presidency. Hence, they began conniving with other *divisionarios*, such as Joaquín Amaro, Oaxaca Governor

Manuel García Vigil, Sinaloa Jefe de Operaciones Angel Flores, and even with those eliminated in prior uprisings such as Diéguez, Alvarado, and Villarreal. Amaro, however, kept Obregón fully informed on the conspiracy to stop Calles.[61] In June 1923, a worried President pointedly warned all *divisionarios* that political discussions by military men on active service could result in severe punishments under Article 545 of the General Orders of the Army.[62]

Obregón's selection of Calles not only alienated the non-Sonoran *divisionarios*, but also brought disharmony to the Sonora clique. The trouble here was that Treasury Minister Adolfo de la Huerta, who had been provisional president following Agua Prieta, had been given to understand that he would succeed Obregón. De la Huerta hesitated for a time before assuming leadership of the 1923 rebellion, but ultimately he bowed to pressures from Obregón's military and civilian opposition. The latter included not only disgruntled labor and agrarian elements, but also middle- and upper-class groups opposed both to the radical Obregón and to the even more extreme Calles.[63]

As in 1920, it was the central government's intervention in a state political dispute, this time in San Luis Potosí, that ignited the rebellion. On August 29, 1923, General Angel Flores, who six months earlier had been stripped of half his troops when Obregón increased the number of military zones and who was not mollified by Obregón's fifty thousand peso allowance to him to study irrigation in Egypt, resigned from the army and declared himself a candidate for the presidency.[64] Calles countered by resigning as Minister of Government and announcing his candidacy. Soon thereafter, Obregón despatched an army under General Luis Gutiérrez to intervene in a disputed gubernatorial election in San Luis Potosí. In response, Obregón's military and civilian opposition pressured de la Huerta into becoming the champion of states rights. He resigned from the cabinet, and in late November declared himself a candidate for the presidency.

The opposition, however, had no illusions about their ability to win the presidency so long as Obregón controlled the election machinery; they knew that victory could only come through use of force. On November 30, the Guerrero Jefe de Operaciones, General Rómulo Figueroa, rose in arms against the government, and his move was seconded in a week by all the anti-Calles *divisionarios*. They took with them into opposition nearly half the army.[65]

One hundred and two generals, one third of those on active duty, backed the rebel movement. The most important ones were Enrique Estrada, Fortunato Maycotte, Manuel García Vigil, Guadalupe Sánchez, Rafael Buelna, Francisco Coss, Angel Flores, Cándido Aguilar, Jesús Augustín Castro, Salvador Alvarado, Antonio Villarreal, Alfonso de la Huerta (brother of Adolfo), and Hipólito Villa (brother of the late Francisco).

As Maycotte happened to be in the capital when the rebellion broke out, he called on Obregón to affirm his loyalty and to demand money and supplies to fight the rebels .The President sent him to War Minister Serrano, who authorized him to draw 100,000 pesos from the National Treasury for campaign expenses. General Juan Gualberto Amaya was with Serrano when Maycotte called, and when the latter left Serrano declared to Amaya, "Maycotte will very soon second the rebel movement." This he did as soon as he left the capital.[66]

Obregón and Estrada, long close friends, aired their differences over the national telegraph. From Guadalajara, Estrada wired Obregón on December 7 that since the President had repeatedly assured him there would be electoral liberty and then arbitrarily had tried to impose Calles, "Tengo el alto honor de desconocer a Alvara Obregón." (I have the high honor of not recognizing Alvaro Obregón.) The following day he received a reply from Obregón excoriating him for being both a "false friend" and a disloyal soldier. Obregón reminded Estrada of the frequent hospitality afforded him at the President's summer place on Lake Chapala, where Estrada was always given the place of honor at the President's table. He ridiculed Estrada's contention that he was fighting to defend the constitution, and charged: "The truth is that your rebellion is engendered by the spirit of your own vanity, which was injured the day [in 1921] when you were relieved by me as Secretary of War and when you prevented my naming you Secretary of Agriculture by giving the press a statement on the agricultural problem that was directly opposed to my agricultural policies . . . and thus your vanity was doubly wounded. I made a mistake in estimating you so highly."[67]

Official statistics reveal that 20 per cent of the officers (102 generals, 573 *jefes,* and 2,417 *oficiales*) and 40 per cent of the troops (23,224) rebelled. This included eighteen infantry battalions, twenty-eight cavalry regiments, two marine battalions and some aviation units. In addition, the army rebels were joined by about 24,000 civilians. Thus, the government initially could count on only 35,000 men to resist the 50,000 rebels.[68] But this numerical disadvantage was nullified within a month as the reserves were pressed into active duty and as thousands of workers and peasants volunteered to defend the Revolution against the "forces of reaction." Obregón astutely publicized the strong *hacendado* support for the rebels and also the active participation in the uprising of so many Carrancista generals over whom "the people" triumphed at Agua Prieta.[69]

Official accounts of the 1923 revolution maintain that it was the people who triumphed over the militarists in the 1923 rebellion. Proletarian volunteers indeed aided the government's cause, but the failure of the rebellion was due as much to the deficiencies of rebel leadership as it was to the effectiveness of loyalist forces.[70] If the rebels had been unified, if their movements had been coordinated, and if they had utilized the element of surprise, they might have toppled Obregón. But such was not the case. Estrada, Maycotte, and Sánchez, rebel commanders in the west, south, and east respectively, had been willing to accept the civilian Adolfo de la Huerta as a political straw man in their resistance to Calles, but they hardly considered him qualified to direct the military campaign. In fact, there were no less than three major rebel movements, none of them coordinated, plus a number of minor ones. On the east coast de la Huerta announced his plan of Veracruz and assumed the title of Jefe Supremo de la Revolución. But Maycotte, ignoring de la Huerta, proclaimed his own plan of Oaxaca. Maycotte declared that the leadership of the rebellion resided exclusively in the hands of Generals Maycotte, Estrada, and Sánchez, who would form a provisional governing junta. Estrada had yet another plan, similar to Maycotte's, while Diéguez, Alvarado, and Aguilar, though they acknowledged the temporary leadership of the "big three," mainly sought advantage for themselves.[71]

Administration forces, led by Obregón, Calles, and Serrano, exploited the divisions in the rebel ranks. Lacking the resources to mount offensives everywhere at once, they attacked first in the east. In December 1923, they took Puebla; in January 1924, they defeated Guadalupe Sánchez at Estación Esperanza, between Veracruz and Puebla. Thereupon they launched their major offensive in the west against Estrada; his army was destroyed in February. The following month, administration forces cleaned out Maycotte in the south and mopped up most of the rebel bands throughout the republic.[72]

One result of the rebellion was elimination from the army of 102 political generals. Estrada, Maycotte, Alvarado, Diéguez, García Vigil, and Buelna were captured and cut down by firing squads, though many lesser generals escaped into exile.[73] However, the rebellion produced more generals than it eliminated. In late 1923, Obregón promoted twenty-three brigadiers and generals of brigade and fifty-four colonels just to make sure they would not defect.[74]

The cost of the three-month 1923-1924 uprising was seven thousand lives and 100 million pesos. The significance of the rebellion was that it sealed the supremacy of the military power of the central government over that of the outlying regions. It spelled the doom of regional caudillism. Also, it strengthened appreciably the labor and peasant counterpoises to the military. "The failure of the 1923 militarist uprising proved the strength of the socialist revolutionaries then in power," wrote Antonio Islas Bravo. "The 1923 fight was not over four years of the presidency but over forty."[75]

SINCE THE CRUSHING of the de la Huerta rebellion made the election and inauguration of General Calles virtual certainties, Obregón was relatively free to spend the last eight months of 1924 in "moralizing the army." Many generals still claimed rewards, which the treasury generally paid, for their services during the rebellion. Claims were usually for private resources expended. General Jaime Carrillo presented a bill for 19,465 pesos, but the average claim for generals was around five thousand pesos. In addition, peasants and workers in arrears in military pay received satisfaction.[76]

The elimination of all the officers involved in the 1923 rebellion did not end all problems of integrity and discipline in the states. Only three months after the rebellion Obregón dismissed several new colonels who had become involved in local corruption. General Fausto Topete reportedly was collecting protection money from the local silver companies and conniving with former officers who had fought for de la Huerta.[77] The Governor of Nayarit complained that the new Jefe de Operaciones, General Anatolio B. Ortega, was terrorizing both the police and the civilians and generally overstepping his authority.[78]

Obregón's campaign to promote professionalism was resumed in 1924. A group of military experts completed work on the new Organic Law for the Army, which provided for orderly recruitment, for regulated training of soldiers, for cadet training for all future officers, and for competitive examinations for all promotions up to the rank of colonel.[79] Reorganization of the army also continued. Nearly all the posts in the table of organization were filled, and every officer was assigned specific military functions.[80] And yet, when Obregón's term ended in December 1924, only a start had been made in building a professional army. This work was to be continued by Obregón's handpicked successor, General Calles.

1925·1937

I V

THE CALLES ERA

THE MAN AND HIS
GOVERNMENT

General Plutarco Elías Calles was the most durable political
personality to emrge from the Revolution. He dominated Mexican politics for a full decade. This achievement was in no
small measure attributable to his success in establishing firm
control over the armed forces, and only when he lost control
did his political power come to an end.

Calles spent the first thirty-five years of life in civilian pursuits. He was a student, a teacher, and a farmer, and, following Madero's triumph, an unsuccessful aspirant for elective
political office. Without any military experience, he took the
field under Obregón to fight Orozco in 1912, Huerta in
1913-1914, Villa in 1914-1915, Carranza in 1920, and de la
Huerta in 1923-1924. He learned tactics on the battlefield and

there displayed superb fighting qualities and great personal valor. Like Obregón, Calles' natural talent for soldiering enabled him to ride the revolutionary wave from colonel to general, to governor, to cabinet minister, and finally to *Jefe Máximo* of the Revolution.

Calles' biographers stress his civilian origin and spirit. They point out that despite his key military role during the years from 1912 to 1924, Calles was really more of a civilian than a militarist; that he disliked uniforms, decorations, and military laurels; that he despised the military caste system and that his heart was always with the working classes. Calles, like Obregón, they argue, chose a career in arms not as an end but as a means to achieve political power and to implement the socialist revolutionary principles to which he was dedicated.[1]

Such were the claims of all the military chieftains of the Revolution. They all posed as representatives of the people, as protectors of the ideals of the Revolution against militarism, and as defenders of social justice and democratic institutions. In all important political disputes, however, the ultimate arbiter was always the army. The one who could sway the bulk of that institution always emerged the victor in political crises. This was just as true of Calles as it had been of Obregón.

By the time he became president, Calles displayed little of the commonness of his fishing-family background or of the mediocrity of his middle-class prerevolutionary calling. His revolutionary experience turned him into a poised and confident ruler who confronted with a mixture of bold deliberation and imperturbable patience the weightiest problems in Mexico—agrarian reform, labor policy, relations with the United States, educational development, the religious question, and the building of a professional army.

Calles was a reformer. Initially, he was more radical and socialistic than Obregón, and under his leadership the Revolution cut more deeply than before. Whereas Obregón's major civilian support had come from the peasants, Calles' main political prop was organized labor. Luis Morones became Minister of Labor, and his CROM, one million strong, began to reap privileges and material benefits from the new "labor president."[2] The agrarians were by no means forgotten, for during Calles' presidential term about seven million acres of land, more than double the amount of Obregón's four years, were redistributed to fifteen hundred peasant villages. In addition, Calles speeded up the rural education program, tripling the number of schools to three thousand, and launched a nationwide public works program, including hospital construction, road building, and general communications development.[3]

Financial support for his social reforms Calles exacted from the propertied elements. Businessmen, both domestic and foreign, were obliged to improve the welfare of their employees, *hacendados* were forced to sell their idle lands at far less than market value and an income tax law obtained revenues from those best able to pay.

President Calles, convinced that the clergy was inimical to the progress of the Revo-

THE ARMY VERSUS THE CHURCH

lution, began to enforce the anticlerical provisions of the 1917 Constitution, particularly Article 3, which required that primary education be secular, and Article 130, which severely limited the number of priests. In 1926, following the public declaration of the Archbishop of Mexico that the Church would resist, Calles closed church schools, turned monasteries into public schools, deported foreign-born priests and nuns, and required all Mexican priests to register with the civil authorities. The clergymen responded by stopping all services, but the government forced them to keep the doors open.

In the impasse between Calles and the Catholic Church, the partisans of both resorted to force. By late 1926 there was violence in Michoacán, Guanajuato, Jalisco, and Colima. Catholic laymen there organized armed bands, the so-called Cristeros, to

83

combat the army. The Cristeros believed that most officers were Masons determined to destroy Catholicism in Mexico.[4] They appealed particularly to the devout Indians of west-central Mexico, and they had twelve thousand men in the field by early 1927. They were led by Generals Enrique Gorostieta and Rodolfo Gallegos, both of whom had been officers in the Federal Army. They appealed to all Catholic officers to help save the nation from "atheistic Bolsheviks."[5] The Cristeros roamed the countryside burning public schools, killing teachers, and dynamiting trains.

Calles responded by ordering National Army units to take the field. For every school burned a church was looted, and for every teacher murdered a priest lost his life. Since the Cristeros were, under the law, "in an ostensible attitude of rebellion against the government," they were generally executed on the spot. The army often hung their Cristero prisoners, one by one, from a line of telephone poles.[6]

The Ejército Nacional was more than a match for the Cristeros. Though sporadic violence continued in the west for several years, the rebellion was brought under control before the

84

end of 1927. Gallegos was slain in battle and Gorostieta was driven into hiding. Thus, the President won out. By meeting force with force he made the Church come to terms. Even the Papacy capitulated; in 1929 it ordered the Mexican clergy to comply with the law and register with the civil authorities.[7]

DURING THE Cristero rebellion, several lesser threats to internal order occurred. The Yaqui Indians of Sonora resisted Calles' agrarian reforms, but they were pacified by General Francisco Manzo's 13,500 troops and by promises of better treatment.[8] In addition, the *defenses sociales*, the agrarian irregulars organized to combat the 1923 revolt, were troublesome and frequently at odds with the regulars, so Calles had the army and police confiscate their weapons.[9] Also, there was bandit activity, local political violence, and sporadic agrarian disturbances, but the scale of such disorders was less than it had been in the early 1920's.

Theimproved **GENERAL JOAQUIN AMARO**
conditions of **REORGANIZES THE ARMY**
internal order
permitted Calles to proceed with a drastic overhaul of the army. The problems were enormous. The War Ministry absorbed more than a third of the budget, more than four times as much as any other ministry. Military expenditures ate up revenues which Calles wanted to spend on public works, education, agriculture and industry. The officers lacked esprit de corps; politics and peculation were still the principal interests of the generals; and the ranks were deficient in discipline, training, and morale.[10]

To tackle these problems, Calles chose General Joaquín Amaro as his Minister of War. A poor Tarascan Indian boy when the fighting began in 1910, Amaro rose rapidly from the ranks as he repeatedly displayed his mettle on the battlefield. He won special recognition in the crucial battle against Villa at Celaya; he won additional laurels in the Agua Prieta uprising;

85

but it was his brilliant role during the de la Huerta rebellion that brought him to the top. He organized strong defensive positions at Puebla to protect Mexico City from assault from the east, and once the rebel strength was decimated in the east and west, he directed the final campaigns against the rebels in the south. Thus it was a soldier of proven military prowess that Calles selected to build the new National Army.[11]

For six years, throughout the administrations of Calles (1924-1928) and Emilio Portes Gil (1928-1930), Amaro was Minister of War. He was the most powerful personality under Calles; inscrutable, taciturn, and tough minded, he was a brilliant organizer and a stern disciplinarian; his methods were often brutal and instantaneous; he reportedly shot and killed a groom for riding one of his polo ponies.[12]

Under instructions from Calles to reduce the military budget, Amaro effected a rigid economy program. He declared a moratorium upon all promotions. He issued an order at the beginning of 1924 granting all generals just two months to justify the rank they claimed, and then rejected all claims of questionable validity.[13] In addition, he reduced the lesser ranks, mustered out most of the irregulars, and placed a 55,000-man limit on regulars.[14] Within three years these actions reduced the military percentage of total budget from 36 per cent to 25 per cent.[15] The burden of the armed forces upon the rest of the economy was further lightened in the late 1920's by making increased use of troops in highway construction and other public works projects.[16]

To provide a proper legal framework for a national army the new War Minister had his legal staff hard at work during 1925 on a new body of military legislation. This was passed by Congress and promulgated as four new general military laws on March 15, 1926.[17] Most important was the new Organic Law which superseded that of 1900. The 1926 law took account of a quarter century of changes and modernization in military organization and practice the world over. In contrast to the 1900 law, that of 1926 specifically set forth the threefold mission of

86

the army "to defend the integrity and independence of the nation, to maintain the constitution, and to preserve internal order." Also formally written into the law were a number of features that had been put into practice by the Carranza and Obregón administrations, such as their reserve, general staff, general inspection, and voluntary enlistment systems.[18]

The 1926 Law of Promotions was designed to end the irregular procedures which had prevailed since 1910. The old law, written in the Díaz era, provided for automatic promotions based on time of service in existing grades—three years for *oficiales,* four years for *jefes* and five years for *generales.* The exigencies of the Revolution, however, wrought havoc with the promotion system. As the Constitutionalist Army swelled during the heavy fighting from 1913 to 1915, hundreds were elevated to generalships on the fields of battle. These were known as *generales de dedo* (finger generals), that is, men whose exalted rank originated from having a finger pointed at them in a battle crisis. Then too, any officer could advance at least one grade by picking the winning side in a rebellion. Thus, as a result of the long revolutionary heritage, the Calles administration found itself with 158 generals for 53,000 men, or one for every 335 men. This was six times the United States Army ratio. There was a similar excess of *jefes.* Under the new law, promotions were no longer automatic but depended upon vacancies in the table of organization. To qualify for such vacancies, which were to be filled by competitive examinations, applicants had to have professional training and active duty experience.[19]

The 1926 Law of Discipline stated that "a career in arms requires that a soldier, in the fulfillment of his duties, sacrifice all personal interests to the sovereignty of the nation, to loyalty toward its institutions, and to the honor of the National Army." Finally, the new Law of Retirement and Pensions specified the legal rewards due all inactives who had fought in some phase of the Revolution, set up a scale of mandatory retirement for those on active duty ranging from forty-five years of age for enlisted men up to seventy for *divisionarios,* provided pensions after twenty years service, and made modest provision for the care of military dependents.[20]

Though the Constitutionalist Army had performed the vital task of destroying the *federales,* the experiences of the Carranza and Obregón administrations clearly exposed the inadequacy of an ad hoc revolutionary army to carry out peacetime military functions. The 1923 uprising had demonstrated the power of regionalism once more, and the problem still remained in the mid-1920's. Hence, the task confronting Calles and Amaro was to build an effective national army. What was needed, no less, was an entirely new body of officers and enlisted men recruited on a national, rather than a regional, basis and trained in military schools designed to make them *bona fide* professionals.

But before such could be provided, a number of revolutionary generals, many of whom were equal or superior in rank to Calles, still had to be dealt with. Obregón, while president, had earned the respect of most *divisionarios* because of his military prestige, but Calles enjoyed no such deference. Most generals had won their right to command on the field of battle, and they regarded their political posts as payment due them for battles won. They viewed their public posts, both political and military, as opportunities for personal gain rather than as obligations to serve their nation.

When Calles became president, there were twenty-one *divisionarios.* Seven were Jefes de Operaciones, five commanded special divisions, two were in the War Ministry, one was a state governor, one a senator, one a diplomat, and four were unassigned. Of the forty *generales de brigada,* twenty-nine were Jefes de Operaciones, two were governors, and two were congressmen. Most of the one hundred *brigadieres* commanded regiments.[21] The most powerful *divisionarios,* in addition to Calles and Amaro, were Eugenio Martínez, Francisco Serrano, Francisco Manzo, Roberto Cruz, Arnulfo Gómez, Gonzalo Escobar, Juan Almazán, Luis Gutiérrez, and Lázaro Cárdenas.

In an attempt to deal with various evils of militarism such as politicking, peculation, venality, and irresponsibility, War Min-

ister Amaro issued the following series of orders: "(1) All those generals and officers who behave scandalously in public places, or without the decorum that their profession demands, will be cashiered regardless of the rank they occupy; (2) Abstain absolutely from carrying out executions of individuals who are not apprehended with arms in hand so that the good name of the army will not be injured . . . by taking upon itself powers that belong only to the ordinary tribunals; [and] (3) Give up politics or resign from the army."[22]

89

Because such orders could only be enforced on those for whom they were not primarily designed, namely, officers below the rank of general, Amaro's peers did not take his reform orders too seriously. The generals continued their drinking and whoring, continued to shoot civilians who happened to incur their displeasure, and continued their political activities. During Calles' first three years of office the familiar complaints accumulated: the Jefe de Operaciones in Baja California was collecting the salaries and food allotments of nonexistent troops; the Jefe de Operaciones of Aguascalientes was menacing the peasant organizations; the Jefe de Operaciones of Guadalajara was enriching himself; the Jefe de Operaciones in Durango was converting towns into "miniature Monte Carlos"; officers in Michoacán were requisitioning livestock, pastures, and dwelling places without settling accounts with the owners.[23]

The methods used by Calles and Amaro to curb the regional commanders were not dissimilar to those previously applied by Díaz and Obregón. That is, they employed a kind of official bribery. Generals were permitted to enrich themselves in exchange for displaying loyalty towards the central government. Military fortunes were not necessarily made illegitimately, but they were made possible as a result of the political influence derived from fighting in the Revolution.

The subject of enrichment by revolutionary generals was investigated by Francisco Naranjo, and the fruits of his research were thirty articles entitled "Los Millionarios de la Revolución," which appeared in the *Diario de Yucatán* (Mérida) during the summer of 1948. According to Naranjo, a number of generals began to accumulate wealth under Carranza—especially Chief of Staff Juan Barragán, son-in-law Cándido Aguilar, and Pablo Gónzalez. Other military fortunes were made during the Obregón administration, but the most notorious military enrichment occurred during the decade of Calles' rule.[24]

Calles himself set an example. As a former school teacher, he had little financial means till the Agua Prieta uprising. As a cabinet officer under Obregón, his situation improved only moderately, but during the decade from 1924 to 1934, when he was President and *Jefe Máximo*, he acquired substantial real estate holdings and considerable liquid wealth. Naranjo estimated Calles' fortune at "no less than twenty million pesos." Amaro was not far behind. When he became War Minister, he sported the finest stable of polo ponies in all Mexico, palatial residences in the capital, and landed estates in the countryside.[25]

Calles and Amaro saw to it that Obregón and his military associates were properly cared for, and Obregón became suddenly prosperous upon retiring from the presidency. With funds borrowed from the national treasury he purchased enough farm machinery to make him one of the largest producers of chickpeas and tomatoes in Sonora. General Francisco Serrano, after being replaced as War Minister by Amaro, gambled away four million pesos in European casinos during the first two years of Calles' administration. General Aarón Sáenz parlayed his close friendship with Obregón and Calles into enough government concessions and contracts to make him one of the wealthiest contractors in Mexico.[26]

High on the list of potentially dangerous generals whom Calles deemed it wise to pamper with financial opportunities was Gonzalo Escobar. He accumulated large sums of money in banks in Torreón and Monterrey, which he used to lead a revolt against Calles in 1929. Juan Almazán not only made a fortune from construction projects and real estate when he was Minister of Public Works and Communications in the late 1920's, but he was also permitted to spend half his time looking after his business enterprises in Mexico City when he was appointed Jefe de Operaciones in his native State of Nuevo León in 1931.[27]

The biggest fortune of all was accumulated by General Abelardo Rodríguez, who served Calles as Governor of Baja California, as War Minister, and as President. In the border towns of Tijuana, Ensenada, and Mexicali, Governor Rodríguez was the principal entrepreneur in the horseracing, casino, and brothel business. Subsequently, he invested in real estate, food processing, stocks, and banking. When he became President in

1932, his fortune was over 100 million pesos. Other generals who became millionares while in public office during the Calles era were Roberto Cruz, Antonio Guerrero, Eulogio Ortíz, Rodrigo Quevedo Moreno, and Miguel N. Acosta.[28]

Generals weren't the only ones to profit. The wealth, the big automobiles, and the high living of Luis Morones and the labor barons were notorious. Civilian officials who became millionaires under Calles included Gobernación Minister Emilio Portes Gil and Public Works Minister Alberto J. Pani. Also, newspaper editor José Manuel Puig Casauranc found the road to fortune paved by friendship with the government.[29] In sum, there was established under Calles a politico-financial cabal not unlike that which existed under Porfirio Díaz at the turn of the century.

PROFESSIONALISM Since military ability generally counted for less than revolutionary zeal in the selection of young officers during the Revolution, Amaro concluded that the political passions of those who had become generals could never be subdued, that he could never sell professionalism to those who had fought so hard to destroy that concept during the years 1910-1915. Hence, his tactic for building a truly national military organization was to bore in from the bottom, to create a corps of young professionals who would one day inherit control of the army.[30]

Those below the rank of *jefe* who continued to display more of a political than a professional interest, Amaro retired. Those *oficiales* willing to train to become serious professionals, he encouraged. Since there were still few officer-training facilities in Mexico, Amaro sent the brightest lieutenants and captains to military academies in France, Spain, Italy, and the United States. He also assigned military attachés to Mexico's embassies in order that they might transmit the latest information relating to modern armies of the world.[31]

Under Obregón the Colegio Militar had degenerated to the point of uselessness. A midsummer, 1925 inspection revealed dirty, littered buildings and grounds with filth everywhere: "horses standing in manure up to their fetlocks, kitchens full of grease and dirt, dining halls with dirty plates and glasses, . . . cadets in sloppy, ragged uniforms,"[32] and officers who had never mounted a horse were in charge of cavalry instruction. Four hundred professors were assigned to train eight hundred cadets. The academy directors, all of them revolutionary generals, were principally interested in political indoctrination, while the ex-*federales,* the only ones with technical military knowledge, were reduced to ineffectivness by suspicions, jealousies, and political purges. The cadets were lacking in morale and deficient in professional application. Most of them were impatient for a rebellion so that promotions would come rapidly. So hopeless was the situation that Amaro closed the Colegio Militar in October 1925, remodeled it, expanded it, and overhauled the staff and curricula.[33] It was reopened in late 1926.

By that time, Amaro was already using young officers who had received training abroad to assist him in building a better general staff. The first step toward this end was the creation in 1926 of a Commission of Military Studies. Out of it was developed the Estado Mayor General (General Staff) of the War Ministry.[34]

The objective of the new training programs was to develop a corps of professionals with a high sense of military dignity and public responsibility. Amaro was determined to change the army from a vehicle for advancing one's political aims into a nonpolitical institution which would restrict itself to the military tasks of defending the nation against internal and external threats. In the young officers he sought to instill a new sense of discipline and of obedience to civil authority.[35]

Once the cadets were commissioned from the newly organized military academy and once selected *oficiales* had been retooled as career-minded professionals, these officers were assigned to regiments of doubtful loyalty, the obvious purpose being to interpose loyal professionals between revolutionary chieftains and their private armies. When these reforms were well advanced in the late 1920's, the next step towards breaking down regional loyalties was taken by shifting commands at ever higher levels of rank.[36] Before the generals could be brought under the control of the central authorities, however, two additional rebellions, those of 1927 and 1929, had to be crushed.

Technical reforms and reorganization were also part of Amaro's program for building a national army. The War Ministry dismissed all civilians and cut its employees by more than one-half. A new table of organization reduced the number of tactical units, and these were made more efficient by technical training programs. The equipment needs of the new army began to be satisfied by imports of arms and of machinery for the new military factories. In line with his modernization program, Amaro created a Military Aviation School in 1930 to train pilots and technicians for a new air force branch of the army. To insure that reform and modernization would be a continuous process, a Comisión Técnica and an Inspección General were established to revise, improve, implement and enforce the new laws and regulations.[37]

Transformation in the training and the way of life for enlisted men was just as sweeping as for the officers. Beginning in 1925, new barracks were built and old ones were reconditioned in accordance with modern concepts of comfort and hygiene. To these installations there now came the new three-year volunteers, of which there was no shortage, to train, to live, and to work. They were issued standard simple uniforms, good shoes, and rifles that would shoot. Their food allowance was no longer pilfered by corrupt *jefes*. Regular haircuts, daily shaving, and frequent changes of underwear were required. Gone from army life were the *soldaderas*, the women who customarily accompanied the troops. Amaro considered them the chief cause of vice, illness, crime, and disorder and hence banned them from all military installations.[38]

Amaro's program kept the troops occupied. They were taught to read and write, and were given technical and tactical training, which was put to practical use against the Yaquis and the

94

Cristeros during 1926 and 1927. New playing fields, modern gymnasiums and a nationwide army sports program provided the troops with physical exercise and recreation. Spare time was spent building roads, laying telegraph lines, repairing railroads, and working on agricultural projects. Amaro also started an enlisted men's weekly, *La Patria,* to boost morale and instill a sense of mission. He sought to make the troops supporters of the central government, protectors of the nation's sovereignty, and defenders of the Revolution.[39]

In addition, Amaro reorganized the rural reserves, the so-called Social Defense Corps which had played such a vital role in the 1923 rebellion. He felt they might be needed again in the future. His objective was to bring them under the control of the central authorities and to end violence in the countryside. To this end he purged the armed peasant organizations of unruly elements and put them under officers who could be depended upon to take their orders from Mexico City.[40]

THE OCTOBER 1927 "REBELLION"

The presidential succession crisis of October 1927 was the first severe test of Amaro's reforms. By early 1926, three years before Calles' term was due to expire, the generals who aspired to succeed him had begun their campaigns. The *divisionarios* made it clear that no civilians would be eligible as candidates for the nation's highest office. Calles had toyed with the notion of having Luis Morones succeed him, but in the face of united opposition from the generals he soon abandoned the idea. For not only did the revolutionary generals feel strongly that civilians had no right to the presidency, but they were also particularly wary of Morones because they feared he might organize labor militias which would ultimately challenge the army.[41]

Amongst the eighteen *divisionarios,* several considered themselves as *presidenciables.* General Arnulfo Gómez felt he had a natural right to succeed Calles because he was the senior officer in the army and considered the presidency as the next logical

95

step in his military career. He was supported by a substantial segment of the army and declared that both Obregón and Calles had assured him that he would be Mexico's next president. He had been engaged in military studies in Europe during 1925, and when he returned to Mexico in early 1926 he was appointed Jefe de Operaciones in Veracruz. From this post he ignored the orders and reform decrees of War Minister Amaro, whom he outranked, and communicated directly with President Calles.[42]

Despite the fact that organized labor opposed Gómez, Calles was for him until late 1926, if for no other reason than the fact that most other *divisionarios* were Obregonistas. The Obregonistas' leading candidate at the time was former War Minister Francisco R. Serrano. Obregón had been impressed by Serrano's brilliance but disturbed by his whoring, drinking, and gambling.[43] Nonetheless, Obregón had long given Serrano the impression that he would be Calles' successor, and he hoped that a study tour in Europe in 1925 would improve his morals.

When Serrano returned to Mexico in the spring of 1926, Calles, hoping to block his candidacy, offered him the post of Minister of Government but Serrano refused.[44] Calles needn't have worried, for Obregón decided that Serrano, whose dissipating had become worse than ever, wouldn't do. He had also decided against Gómez, whom he considered a Callista.

By the fall of 1926, Obregón had made up his mind that he himself was the only suitable *presidenciable,* and that his services were indispensable for carrying on the Revolution; accordingly, he informed Calles of his decision. Calles added up the power factors—most of the *divisionarios* were Obregonistas and so were the agrarians—and decided not to make the challenge.[45] He dropped Gómez and came out for Obregón, assuming, no doubt, that he might again succeed Obregón later.

The Constitution of 1917 specified that presidents and ex-presidents were ineligible for reelection, but Calles removed this legal impediment by a November 1926 congressional amendment to the Constitution which permitted the reelection of an ex-president providing he had been out of office for one full term. For good measure, the military and agrarian forces supporting Obregón induced Congress to extend the presidential term from four to six years.

Many were upset over this sacrifice of legal principle, which smacked of the Díaz system of *continuismo, alternación,* and *imposición* against which the Revolution had been fought. But none were more furious than Gómez and Serrano; both decided to challenge Obregón.

In early 1927, Calles' apprehension about a possible succession crisis was reflected in his severe crackdown on army political activity. On January 13, twenty-seven soldiers who attacked an army post in Oaxaca were put before the firing squad by direct orders from Calles.[46] On April 7, Amaro again warned all officers to "give up politics or resign from the army."[47] This prompted Gómez and Serrano to take the six months' leave required by the Constitution if they were to make themselves eligible for the presidency, and in June 1927 they both declared their candidacies. As soon as they were out of the service, however, Amaro made political use of service organs to condemn them. The May 1927 issue of the *Revista del Ejército* reprinted a *Universal* editorial condemning the political ambitions of

97

Gómez and Serrano;[48] the July 9, 1927, issue of *La Patria* carried a headline editorial denouncing Gómez's "Bando Conservador" for attempts to involve the army in its reactionary cause. The press in Mexico City also censured the large number of officers who took leave to campaign for Gómez and Serrano.[49] Those Gómez and Serrano partisans who did not take leave were relieved of their commands and transferred to innocuous desk jobs.

Since Obregón was the official candidate, no officer found it necessary to take leave to campaign for him. Furthermore, the votes of the peasants, through the National Agrarian Party, were assured him, and although urban labor initially favored Serrano, the CROM had no alternative but to accept Obregón once Calles proclaimed him the official candidate.[50]

Though the overwhelming power of the government and the revolutionary masses were aligned against them, Gómez and Serrano worked inside constitutional channels for three months. Behind Gómez was the Partido Nacional Revolucionario, an anti-reelectionist group organized by Vito Alessio Robles. Gómez defended the 1917 Constitution, and denounced both Calles and Obregón for violating it.[51]

Serrano, like Gómez and like Obregón, proclaimed himself the only candidate who stood for the principles of the Revolution. He sought support from both capital and labor, promising all things to all men, and repeatedly accused Obregón of breaking a promise to back him for the presidency. Serrano's campaign was astutely managed by General Carlos A. Vidal, but the candidate damaged his own cause by continuing his carousing in the capital. One night, while in a state of inebriation, he reportedly embraced a waitress in front of the Teatro Lírico.[52]

With the government in control of the election machinery, Gómez and Serrano realized by September 1927 that they had no chance of winning without resorting to violence. It may be that they had this in mind from the beginning. They were adventurous men who preferred to test their strength in battle rather than at the polls. They considered it more *macho* (manly) to overthrow the government, and they were not afraid to risk their lives in the process. Serrano's advisors suggested arresting Calles and shooting Obregón, but Serrano insisted on challenging them on the battlefield.[53]

The plan was for Gómez to rise with his army in Veracruz while Serrano did the same in Cuernavaca. But timing and coordination were bad, and Calles and Obregón anticipated the uprisings. They ordered all the conspirators arrested and shot. This was the fate of Serrano, Carlos Vidal, and their followers in Cuernavaca on October 3. During the following month a number of Serranista and Gomecista officers were killed in small uprisings scattered throughout Mexico. Gómez initially escaped, but he too was captured and shot on November 5.[54] The rebellion was crushed in little more than a month.

In the emergency the agrarian reserves were mobilized. They handled a few local uprisings, such as that of General Alberto Salazar in Torreón—he and all of his two hundred followers were executed—but the army was sufficiently loyal so that this second line of defense was not really needed.[55] Whereas in 1923 nearly half the army supported the rebel movemnt, in 1927 considerably less than a quarter did. Amaro's reorganization and reform program had successfully met the first test. The army, despite the defection of twenty-eight generals, had sustained the government.[56] All opposition candidates had been eliminated and Obregón was elected president.

THE SUCCESSION CRISIS

July 17, 1928
April 1929

The July 1, 1928 election of Obregón, the nation's most powerful general and popular politician, pointed toward stability. Disloyal elements were purged from the army during the 1927 rebellion, the agrarians backed the president-elect, and although Morones and the CROM broke with Obregón during the campaign, Obregón still retained considerable urban labor support. Mexico, it seemed, could look forward to at least a half dozen years of political calm.

These expectations were rudely upset by the July 17, 1928 assassination of Obregón by a religious fanatic. Stunned Obregonistas variously blamed the clergy, Morones' henchmen, and even the Callistas. In the disturbed aftermath of the assassination, the crucial political issue became the loyalty of the Jefes de Operaciones. The whole nation breathed easier as they began to telegraph, one by one, their assurances of support for Calles for the four and one-half months that remained of his term.[57] Protection of the military chieftains' dominant position vis-a-vis the restless civilian elements dictated a stance of momentary unity and loyalty toward Calles. Even though the generals' interim attitude was one of restrained vigilance, they fully expected to determine amongst themselves who Mexico's next president would be.

The political genius of Calles was never better displayed than in the resolution of this crisis. His September 1, 1928, State of the Union message was certain to deal with the succession problem, and all the revolutionary generals descended upon the capital to hear it. As they were lined up behind Calles when he delivered his speech to Congress, it seemed obvious to those present that it would be necessary for Calles to appease the ambitious military chieftains. Instead Calles made a bold attempt to reduce their political power. He declared that Mexico should seize the present opportunity to exchange its unstable caudillo political tradition for a more peaceful, productive, and civilized system of government by people, constitutions, and laws. He concluded his address by declaring that in the effort to make such a transition "I establish myself as the guarantor of the noble and disinterested conduct of the army."[58] What Calles was saying, indirectly, was that generals were no longer necessary for governing Mexico and this notion was loudly applauded by Congress and by the galleries.[59]

But serious questions remained. Would Congress, controlled by the Obregonistas, be allowed to choose Calles' successor? Would the generals insist on making this decision? Would Calles himself retain power by designating his own man?

It soon became apparent that, despite Calles' plea, the final decision on the succession problem would be made by the military. For immediately following his address, Calles held a secret meeting with the thirty ranking generals at the Hotel Regis. Here he cautioned them that if army leaders vied for the presidency it would prove disastrous not only for themselves and their institution, but for the nation as well. Several uniformed *presidenciables* had already made their bids, notably ranking *divisionarios* Gonzalo Escobar and Juan Almazán, Coahuila Governor Manuel Pérez Treviño, and Aarón Sáenz, who had been Obregón's campaign manager. If they persisted in their aspirations, warned Calles, the country faced another bloody rebellion.[60]

Four days later, on September 5, the generals met again in the Presidential Palace. Here Calles made two specific proposals: "(1.) That no army officer should become either provisional or permanent president, since not only would this give the Mexican people a bad impression of the army, but also it would split the army into rival factions and lead to violence; (2.) That the army and the Congress, which would make the final selection, must agree beforehand on a candidate so that the stability of the government and the Revolution itself might be preserved."[61]

While these arguments for corporate self-interest made sense to the generals, they by no means conceded that they were not the best qualified to govern. At the meeting Almazán declared: "I deem any *divisionario* more able to occupy the presidency than any civilian," and his colleagues agreed unanimously. But the profusion of military candidates left the generals little choice but to bow to expediency and allow a civilian to succeed Calles. Since they could not agree on who should be president, they agreed that none should—at least for the moment. But they did insist on deciding which civilian should have the office. Emilio Portes Gil, the Minister of Government, was their choice, and they instructed Calles to guide Congress toward this selection.[62] On September 25, 1928, Congress unanimously elected Portes Gil the provisional president.[63]

What was not generally realized at the time, either by the generals or the Obregonista Congress, was that the real winner in the selection of Portes Gil was none other than Calles. Despite repeated public assurances that he was retiring from politics, Calles had no such intentions. What he had done was to impose his own man, and through him he continued to rule Mexico.

One final stroke of political genius by Calles came in late 1928 when he issued a public plea for all generals to remain at their posts until after Portes Gil took office, thereby displaying their loyalty to the new administration. The real reason for this plea, however, was to put the generals on the spot. If they remained on active duty through November of 1928, then they would be constitutionally ineligible as candidates for the permanent presidency to be filled in 1929. To have resigned or taken leave before the end of November, after Calles urged them not to, would have been tantamount to a confession of selfish political ambition and a lack of concern for defense of the Revolution.[64]

On December 1, 1928, the day his term expired, Calles founded the Partido Nacional Revolucionario (PNR). Its first important task would be to select a permanent president. Calles' aim in creating the PNR was to establish a formal code of political succession and thus put an end to battlefield contests for the presidency. He also hoped that a formal party structure would create an accepted principle of legitimacy and end the necessity of maintaining one's self in power by use of force.[65] Though Calles resigned from the presidency of the PNR soon after organizing it, his power in no way diminished since he continued to control PNR leaders Portes Gil, Sáenz, and Pérez Treviño.

The first PNR convention began its deliberations in Querétaro on March 1, 1929. The nine hundred delegates were supposed to equally represent the three principal interest groups of the Revolution, but labor's factional strife and the agrarian forces' lack of cohesion assured the military of the dominant voice. The most powerful generals were Lázaro Cárdenas of Michoacán, Saturnino Cedillo of San Luis Potosí, Abelardo Rodríguez of Sonora, Maximino Avila Camacho of Puebla, and Juan Almazán of Nuevo Léon. Though Calles was able to bar them as candidates for the presidency, these regional military leaders had no intention of surrendering their power to the central government. Calles failed in his attempts to impose Aarón Sáenz because the Obregonista generals now considered Sáenz a renegade, but he got them to accept General Pascual Ortíz Rubio, Mexican ambassador to Brazil.[66]

A number of generals felt duped by Calles, but Amaro kept these under close observation and tried to control them by shifting their commands. If they resisted, he began infiltrating Callista *oficiales* and troops into their *jefaturas* (military districts). The principal dissidents were Generals Gonzalo Escobar (disgruntled over not being named War Minister), Jesús M. Aguirre (Jefe de Operaciones in Sonora), Marcelo Caraveo (Governor of Chihuahua), Roberto Cruz (backed by the CROM), Francisco Urbalejo, Claudio Fox, and Fausto Topete. All these generals accused Calles of perverting the Revolution by *personalismo*. By early 1929, their political decline became public knowledge when the government did not invite them to the PNR convention.[67]

The generals' only hope for avoiding ignominious retirement and complete political eclipse was rebellion. Consequently, in February 1929, they drew up their Plan of Hermosillo, creating the Ejército Renovador de la Revolución under the command of Escobar. They invited all Mexicans to join them in protesting Obregón's assassination and in resisting Calles' tyranny.[68] They launched their rebellion on March 3, 1929, just after the PNR convention opened.

The 1929 uprising was far more serious than that of 1927. Nearly a third of the officers and thirty thousand troops rebelled. The fighting lasted two and one-half months, during which time more than two thousand died in battle.[69] Calles

103

assumed the post of War Minister and directed the campaign against the rebels. The agrarian forces were again mobilized, and, as in 1923, they played a vital role in crushing the rebellion. Another factor in the government's victory was the superiority of its modern tactics and equipment.[70] Never again, following their defeat in 1929, were the political generals of the Revolution able to mount a serious challenge to the central authorities. As in 1927, all the rebel generals were either shot or exiled, and a purge of the army again took place. His military job completed, Calles returned to his self-created political post of *Jefe Máximo de la Revolución* and continued as Mexico's strong man for another six years.

1929
1934
THE MILITARY AND POLITICS DURING THE "SEXENIO" The political power of the top revolutionary generals was never more overwhelming than during the *Sexenio,* when a cabal of five *divisionarios* ruled Mexico through puppet Presidents Portes Gil (1928-30), Ortiz Rubio (1930-1932), and Abelardo Rodríguez (1932-1934). Calles was indeed the strongest general but he shared his power with four others. The "big five" were Calles, War Minister Amaro, Governors Cedillo of San Luis Potosí and Cárdenas of Michoacán, and Almazán. A secondary foursome, all of them heroes of the 1929 rebellion, included Eulogio Ortiz, Miguel Acosta, Alejandro Monge, and Matías Ramos.

The new military unity produced political calm. Following the Escobar rebellion, military opposition to the central government remained insignificant for half a dozen years. The various War Ministers (Amaro under President Portes Gil, Calles under Ortiz Rubio, and Cárdenas under Rodríguez) dealt summarily with the disloyal and the politically ambitious. For example, in the spring of 1929, Amaro removed three generals from the War Ministry staff for political activity.[71] Two years later Calles frequently shifted the Jefes de Operaciones, ostensibly "with the end of giving them opportunity to acquire a broad knowledge of the National Territory and of the desires of the army," as President Ortiz Rubio explained,[72] but actually for the purpose of eliminating personal loyalties of troops to their commanders. After the Escobar rebellion, the nearest thing to a military revolt during the *Sexenio* was the October 1933 plot of nine young professional officers to seize control of the army and force the revolutionary officers into retirement. The conspirators had been frustrated in their expectations for pay and promotion by the reduced size and budget of the army. After the plot was discovered, all nine were dismissed from the service.[73]

Following this minor scare, the *divisionarios* sponsored a December 27, 1933 amendment to army regulations which provided that any officer who had participated in a rebellion and had been discharged could never again enter the service. It further provided that no one could be removed from the army except for disloyalty to the government. The amendment was obviously designed to insure lifetime tenure for the generals of the Revolution by imposing maximum penalties for any challenge to their superior rank and authority.[74]

Though President Portes Gil repeatedly maintained that he was independent of the military, his policies were identical with those of the military. This made it evident that even for his brief provisional tenure of office, Portes Gil depended upon the sufferance of the *divisionarios*. They resented taking orders from a civilian, and were impatient to get rid of Portes Gil.[75]

The military direction and control of Mexican politics during the *Sexenio* was asserted largely through the PNR, where the military continued to overshadow the agrarian and labor sectors. Calles had favored Portes Gil for the presidency, not only to prevent a rival general from taking the office, but also to reduce the long-standing agrarian hostility to himself. By mollifying Obregonista Generals Sáenz and Pérez Treviño with high PNR posts, he was able to split the agrarian political organization, bring the moderates under his control, and leave the extremists without government support.[76]

The CROM was not even encouraged by the military chieftains to join the PNR, and Morones, a personal enemy of Portes Gil, had no desire to join. With Calles' approval—more correctly, at his instigation—Portes Gil encouraged anti-CROM labor groups, which were made dependent upon the government and placed in a subordinate position inside the PNR.[77] Portes Gil declared shortly after his election that Morones and the CROM were washed up politically "because the army has always been unfriendly to them."[78]

The November 17, 1929, elections pitted Brigadier General Pascual Ortiz Rubio, the PNR candidate, against former Education Minister José Vasconcelos, the Anti-Reelectionist candidate. Vasconcelos, a civilian, charged that the army was much too large for Mexico's real needs and called for a sharp reduction of military expenditures. But Ortiz Rubio defended the existing establishment as necessary to defend the Revolution against domestic and foreign enemies. In the elections, Vasconcelos was awarded only 5 per cent of the total vote, whereupon he charged fraud, announced his Plan of Guaymas, and called on the people to take up arms against the government. Since only one general and a few troops supported him, Vasconcelos was forced to flee into exile.[79]

President Ortiz Rubio did not belong to the ruling military cabal. He was only a general of brigade. He had joined the Revolution in 1910, but over the years he had made his reputation as an engineer. Under Carranza he had served as governor of his native state of Michoacán; in 1920 he joined the Agua Prieta uprising, and later he served as Obregón's Secretary of Communications and Public Works. Under Calles he held various diplomatic posts, and when he was recalled from Brazil to accept the PNR nomination, he was relatively unknown. Ortiz Rubio was even more of a puppet than Portes Gil, and the "big five" continued to rule. Amaro and Calles served successively as War Minister, and Almazán as Minister of Communications and Public Works during Ortiz Rubio's presidency. Other generals in the cabinet included Pérez Treviño as Minister of Agriculture, and Sáenz as Minister of Education.

The exclusive power of the "big five" became apparent in a number of ways. After Ortíz Rubio was inaugurated, Calles made Portes Gil President of the PNR. But when Portes Gil expounded ideas about building broader civilian participation in the PNR, (which Amaro opposed), and tried to build a political following of his own in the northeast, (where Calles had reserved the governorships for his own sons), Cárdenas, in October 1930, replaced Portes Gil as PNR President.[80] Cárdenas thereupon stepped up the attack upon Morones and the CROM by encouraging all anti-CROM labor elements to seek political shelter under the PNR roof, and at the same time barred CROM unions from membership. In the process organized labor became more and more dependent upon the military.

Calles meanwhile ran roughshod over the agrarians. The adverse economic consequences of the great depression changed Calles' mind in 1930 about the wisdom of further land redistribution, and he ordered the state governors, half of whom were military men, to slow down agrarian reform. Three civilian governors who delayed carrying out Calles' orders were ousted not only from their government posts but also from the PNR, and their political careers were thereby ruined forever.[81] By the end of 1932, the land reform clauses of the 1917 Constitution were virtually a dead letter. And how were the agrarians controlled? The extremists were simply dropped by the PNR, and the regional agrarian confederations were destroyed in 1932 when Calles reorganized the PNR upon hierarchical lines much like the army itself.[82]

The military was supreme both in the government and the official party. The bureaucrats, all of whom were required to contribute annually seven days pay to the PNR, were as dependent upon the military as the workers and peasants. Government posts and party posts overlapped, with the hierarchy in both dominated by military chieftains. Generals controlled both the executive branch of government and the PNR executive committee. In 1931, for example, they held half the governorships and such key cabinet posts as War (Calles), Government

(Cárdenas), Agriculture (Cedillo), and Communications and Public Works (Almazán).[83]

Although labor and agrarian extremists were eliminated, the PNR by no means became reactionary. Calles continued to harass the Church and Cárdenas kept rightist elements out of the party. The military, however, were so dominant during the *Sexenio,* that they did not even feel abliged to seek civilian support. They acted autonomously.[84]

For a year after his inauguration, Ortiz Rubio apparently was content to occupy the office of president without assuming power, to await orders from Calles, and to ratify decisions privately made by the *Jefe Máximo* and the other four *divisionarios.* After a time, however, he became restless in the face of growing public ridicule and impetuously appointed two of his own supporters to public office. The *divisionarios* thereupon refused to serve, the President's position then became untenable, and he resigned on September 2, 1932. The next day Congress, following instructions from the "big five," named War Minister Abelardo Rodríguez to serve the remaining two years of Obregón's original six-year presidential term.[85]

Although Rodríguez was a *divisionario* he was not accepted as a member of the ruling cabal. As indicated, he had made a fortune while Governor of Baja California. During the early 1930's, Calles brought him to the capital where he served with distinction under Portes Gil and Ortiz Rubio as Sub-Secretary of War, as Minister of Commerce, Industry, and Labor, and as Minister of War. As President, Rodríguez wisely confined himself to routine administration rather than policy making, and thus he got along well with his benefactors. Cárdenas served as his War Minister and Calles remained *Jefe Máximo.*[86]

During Rodríguez's two years in office Calles' power began to wane. First of all, his health was not good, and he could not devote full attention to affairs of state. Then too, he had the utmost confidence in Rodríguez's abilities to look after and uphold his interests. As a consequence, Calles spent much of his time in Cuernavaca and Baja California.

Although the PNR initially had concentrated power in Calles' hands, as the party became more institutionalized the expanding bureaucracy inside it began to develop interests of its own and to assume a less dependent position.[87] This same trend toward self-assertion and independence occurred in the labor and agrarian sectors. Hitherto amorphous urban labor groups found strength in a new federation formed in 1933 under the leadership of Vicente Lombardo Toledano. They complained that the military were not paying adequate attention to the needs and wishes of organized labor. Also in 1933, as Mexico began to recover from the shock of the world depression, the agrarians protested that the principles of the Revolution were being ignored, and they demanded that agrarian reform be resumed. In general, civilian interest groups began to challenge the military leadership.

But the more immediate threat to Calles himself, though he did not fully realize it at the time, was from Cárdenas. Calles planned to install another military puppet in the presidency, such as General Pérez Treviño or Colonel Riva Palacio, following the expiration of Rodríguez's term. He was prevented from doing this because Cárdenas, as Minister of War under Rodríguez, had by his policies, speeches, and reforms succeeded in winning over the junior officers and enlisted men. In addition, labor and agrarian elements were attracted by his radicalism. In fact, so much military and popular support developed in behalf of Cárdenas during 1933 that it would have been difficult for Calles to bypass him. Calles still felt he could control him. Meanwhile, during late 1933 and the first half of 1934, Calles began to rebuild his political strength by yielding to some of the demands of urban labor, reviving the land redistribution program, and by inaugurating a liberal agrarian credit program.[88]

The *divisionarios* did not utilize their pre-eminent political positions during the *Sexenio* to enhance unduly the institutional interests of the army. On the contrary they recognized **MILITARY AFFAIRS 1929-1934**

109

that the army was larger than necessary and that its budgetary demands were too great a drain on the hardpressed economy during the depression of the early 1930's. Accordingly, the military reduced its budgetary demands by one-third between 1930 and 1933, whereas the total national budget dropped by only one-sixth. The military portion of the total budget dropped from 32 per cent in 1930 to 25 per cent in 1933.[89]

The army curbed unnecessary expenditures. The August 1931 government salary reductions of 10 to 15 per cent affected military as well as civilian employees. Just prior to this, the customary double salaries for officers holding positions in the nonmilitary branches of government were abolished.[90] Spending on barracks construction and equipment was curbed sharply during the years 1930-1932. In early 1933, War Minister Cárdenas suspended recruiting, prohibited activation of reserves, reduced the number of regiments, and donated surplus cavalry horses to needy peons.[91] Meanwhile the army assumed a larger burden than ever in public works, especially road building and road maintenance, and in disaster relief work.[92]

Despite budgetary tightening, professional development was not permitted to lag. In the enlisted sector, the emphasis was placed upon education. Special efforts were made to raise the intellectual and cultural level of the troops. Inside the War Ministry a new education section, ultimately to become the Dirección General de Educación Militar, was formed. The goals of educating the soldiers were expanded beyond mere literacy to include technical training that could be useful later in civilian life.[93]

Indoctrination of the enlisted men in their responsibilities as guardians of the Revolution was stepped up. *El Nacional*, the PNR mouthpiece, repeatedly reminded the soldiers that they were the sustainers of the ideals of the Mexican proletariat. Rodríguez declared the "armed citizenry" responsible for "carrying out the postulates of the Revolution," while Cárdenas proclaimed the soldier "a preponderant factor in our revolutionary life and a sustainer of the conquests of the Mexican people."[94]

For the officer corps emphasis was also placed upon training and education. Again Amaro played a key role here, for when Calles replaced him as War Minister in 1931, Amaro became the Director of Military Education. In 1932 he founded the Escuela Superior de Guerra (War College). Here the brightest young professionals, selected by competitive examinations, received three years of specialized training for general staff positions and command posts.[95] In addition, promising young officers continued to be sent to the best military schools in Western Europe to acquire knowledge for improving their own military establishment. To the latter end, Amaro established special schools of application for infantry, artillery, cavalry, and engineering officers.[96]

During 1929 there was a great deal of discussion in military circles about another reorganization of the army. Key issues included the role of agrarian irregulars, obligatory versus voluntary service, and possible establishment of a national guard.[97] The actual reorganization did not begin, however, until President Rodríguez got special powers from Congress on December 23, 1932, to legislate on all War Ministry matters, independently of Congress, for the period January 1 to August 1, 1933. This is when War Minister Cárdenas established the Servicio de Intendencia to promote sound accounting procedures and better fiscal management, reorganized the Inspección General to see that military law and regulations were more closely observed, and set up the Dirección General de Materias de Guerra to handle arms and equipment acquisitions. In addition, Cárdenas streamlined, as well as reduced in number, the cavalry, infantry, and artillery regiments, and created a new Department of Engineers.[98]

In sum, the military establishment became more professional and less political during the *Sexenio*. These changes occurred primarily in the ranks and in the junior officer corps. The generals, however, continued to be interested primarily in politics.

1934·1940

V

THE CÁRDENAS ERA

CARDENAS BECOMES THE
STRONGMAN 1934-1936

Lázaro Cárdenas was born in Michoacán in 1895. Because
his parents were modest property owners Lázaro may be considered middle class. He attended elementary school, then
worked in a tax office and a paint shop, and joined the Constitutionalist Army in 1913. During the years from 1915 to 1916
he fought under Calles, advancing to the rank of colonel. In
1920, then a brigadier general, he joined the Agua Prieta rebellion. In the early 1920's he served as Jefe de Operaciones in
Veracruz and Michoacán, and he fought against de la Huerta
in 1923. He displayed unwavering loyalty to Calles in the rebellions of 1927 and 1929. He served as Governor of Michoacán in 1929, as President of the PNR in 1930, and as War
Minister in 1933.

Cárdenas was a member of the *divisionario* clique which ruled Mexico during the *Sexenio*. An uneasy peace prevailed amongst the "big five" because of conflicting ideologies and personal ambitions. Each of them wanted to be president, except Calles, who preferred a puppet president. Amaro and Almazán had become progressively more conservative as the Revolution progressed during the 1920's, whereas Cedillo and Cárdenas had become more radical. Calles took advantage of the conflicts of the other four to enhance his own position.

During 1930, Calles was understandably disturbed by rumors that War Minister Amaro was planning to assassinate him and take over the government, and though he publicly scoffed at the rumors and praised Amaro as a "model and loyal soldier," he assumed the post of War Minister himself. Amaro headed a clique of conservative generals who were greatly concerned that Calles did nothing to curb the aggressive agrarianism of Governors Cedillo of San Luis Potosí and Cárdenas of Michoacán.[1] Calles recognized Almazán's military and political influence, but he was never close to him personally. Furthermore, Calles had oscillated on the social reform issue, being radical in the late 1920's, conservative in the early 1930's, then radical again just prior to the 1934 elections.

Cárdenas' candidacy split the high command of the army, for when he resigned as War Minister to run for the presidency, a number of generals took leave to campaign for him.[2] The most powerful of these were Cedillo, whose radicalism matched that of Cárdenas, and Almazán, whose practical considerations overcame his ideological convictions. Though PNR head Pérez Treviño aspired to the presidency himself, after Cárdenas won the party nomination, he joined the Cardenista army clique, and so did Sáenz.[3] But the basic loyalties of most generals still remained with Calles.

The election of Cárdenas was the least disturbing in Mexico's revolutionary history.[4] His only opponents were General Antonio Villarreal of the Anti-Reelectionist Party and Colonel Adalberto Tejada of the Radical Socialist Party. The official tabulation showed two and one-quarter million votes for Cárdenas and forty thousand for his two opponents. There were the usual cries of fraud, and there were rumors that Villarreal and Pablo González would launch a rebellion from Texas, but nothing happened. On December 1, 1934, Cárdenas assumed the presidency.[5]

Cárdenas' first months in office went smoothly because he accepted a Callista cabinet, including Calles' son Rudolfo as Minister of Communications and Public Works and General Pablo Quiroga as War Minister. The only Cardenista in the cabinet was Minister of Economy General Francisco Mújica. Callista General Matías Ramos was made head of the PNR.

When Calles left for medical treatment in Los Angeles, however, Cárdenas became more independent. Contrary to Calles' wishes, he launched a program of social reform. He began to expropriate lands for distribution to peasant villages and encouraged urban labor to assert itself and strike for its rights, if necessary. The result was rising tension and unrest in Mexico during the spring of 1935 as the landed and business elements resisted this sudden deepening of the Revolution. A by-product of this rightist resistance was the Fascist "Gold Shirt" organization, headed by former Villista General Nicolás Rodríguez, whose members began to clash with labor and agrarian forces in the streets of the capital.[6]

Cárdenas' radicalism also disturbed the army. Most generals, more conservative than the President, took a dim view of Cárdenas' proposal to arm the peasants and of his close cooperation with Marxist labor leader Vicente Lombardo Toledano. Several high-ranking generals, including Calles and Abelardo Rodríguez, were financially hurt by the government's closing of gambling houses. And General Amaro, the Director of Military Education, was attacked by the President for alleged favoritism in granting diplomas.[7]

To counter the alienation of the generals, Cárdenas catered to the junior officers and the troops. He sponsored better schools, housing facilities, and pensions. He increased the uniform allowances for *oficiales,* was liberal in awarding medals and decorations, and he reminded the men in the ranks of their peasant and labor origins and of their consequent social obligation to be loyal to his pro-labor, pro-agrarian government.[8]

When Calles returned to Mexico City in May 1935, he conferred with his principal supporters. These still included most of the generals, the cabinet, about half the congressmen, most business leaders, over half the principal PNR officials, and a minority of the peasant and labor leaders. The Callistas decided that Cárdenas had to be stopped lest the Revolution fall into the hands of irresponsible extremists. So, on June 12, 1935, Calles issued a "patriotic declaration" to the press, in which he condemned labor strikes and agrarian violence and warned Cárdenas to clamp down lest Mexico's future be endangered.[9]

Cárdenas, however, felt confident of enough backing to ignore the voice that had been decisive in Mexican politics for a full decade. His supporters included a minority of the generals and *jefes,* a large majority of the *oficiales* and enlisted men, about half of the civilian politicians, most labor leaders, and nearly all the agrarians.[10]

Cárdenas' response to Calles' warning was to remove all the Callistas from the cabinet. The new Minister of Agriculture became General Saturnino Cedillo, whose Catholic faith appealed to the anti-Callista Church and whose private army of twenty thousand could be useful in fighting a possible Callista rebellion. General Andrés Figueroa replaced Pablo Quiroga as War Minister and immediately began removing the Callista generals from key command posts. Portes Gil replaced General Matías Ramos as head of the PNR and promptly removed all top Callista officials. General Mújica was assigned the important Communications and Public Works post and General Eduardo Hay was appointed Foreign Minister.[11]

These changes were made so rapidly that Calles, caught off guard, had no chance to resist. A beaten man, he returned to California "for reasons of health." Shortly thereafter, the purge of Callistas in the middle and lower echelons of the officer corps,

116

the PNR, the labor unions, and the agrarian organizations began. In addition, the Cardenistas took control of Congress and through efficient use of the election and patronage machinery reduced the Callistas to insignificance.

The substitution of the followers of one caudillo with those of another throughout the bureaucracy and the PNR proved to be a process which produced widespread dissatisfaction. While the administration rationalized its purges with charges of corruption and incompetence, the Callistas demanded a hearing. Calles saw an opportunity for a comeback in this situation, and on December 13, 1935, he returned to the capital, along with Luis Morones, to defend himself and his supporters against slander and vilification. The net result of his protests was that many Callistas who had only been transferred from positions of influence to innocuous posts were now entirely removed from government employment. For the "crime" of greeting Calles at the airport, Generals Amaro (Director of Military Education), Manuel Medinaveytia (Jefe de Operaciones of the Valley of Mexico), Pedro Almada (Jefe de Operaciones of Verucruz), and José María Tapia were relieved of their commands. In addition, five Callista senators were expelled from Congress for "seditious and rebellious" activities. Cárdenas declared these stern moves necessary because "a conspiracy is being carried on against the government of the republic by those whose political interests were injured by the breaking-off of political relationships between Calles and the government."[12]

The positions of Calles and Morones became untenable thereafter. As they continued to speak about the threat of communism in Mexico, Cárdenas curbed their political activities and harrassed them in the courts on charges of corruption. Meanwhile, mass demonstrations, spurred by Cárdenas' accusations, were organized to demand the expulsion of Calles from the country. Following the early April 1936 bombing of the Mexico City-Veracruz train, Morones and Calles were charged with responsibility for the crime and packed off into exile by orders of Cárdenas. With them were sent Generals Melchor Ortega, former Governor of Guanajuato, and José María Tapia. On May 1, Cárdenas invited back from exile those generals and civilian politicians previously ousted by Calles and Obregón. Thus ended the politico-military hegemony of Sonoran generals which had prevailed since 1920.[13]

What explains the collapse of Callismo? Certainly its conservatism was ill-suited to the growing popular demands for social justice. Then too, the material gains afforded revolutionary generals transformed many of them from politicians into businessmen who were unwilling to risk their wealth by supporting Calles in the 1935 crisis. Also, Cárdenas profited politically from Calles' long feud with the Church and from the support of the many enemies, both military and civilian, which Calles had made. Finally, there was Cárdenas himself, whose sudden emergence from political obscurity had a most exhilarating effect upon the development of his political intelligence and energy.

Cárdenas' victory over Calles only destroyed the aggressively Callista segment of the military. The generals of the revolution still considered it their right and duty to manage the Mexican nation. Cárdenas still faced the task of removing the army from politics.

1935 1939 DEVELOPMENT OF THE ARMY A vital segment of Cárdenas' program for deepening and purifying the Revolution was the reform and reorganization of the army. The goals of his Plan Sexenio Militar were (1) "the moral and professional advance of the army" and (2) "the organic betterment of the military institution."[14]

The spur to professionalism came through the President's implementation of recommendations made by the Commission of Military Studies. In 1935 he ordered proficiency tests for all infantry officers below the rank of *jefe,* and those who failed to measure up to minimum standards of military expertise were required to take remedial training. On April 16, 1936, he decreed that professional merit, as demonstrated in competitive examin-

118

ations, was the sole criterion for promotion of officers below the rank of *jefe*. At the same time, he reduced officers' normal career spans from thirty-five years to twenty-five and thus provided for more rapid retirement of the officers of the Revolution. The age limits on active service were henceforth forty-eight for *oficiales*, fifty-eight for *jefes*, and sixty-five for *divisionarios*. In 1937, the President proclaimed part-time civilian employment incompatible with active duty status,[15] and simultaneously saw to it that officers had sufficient incomes so that outside employment would be unnecessary. In 1935, he increased their uniform and equipment allowances, and two years later he raised their pay by 10 per cent. In addition, officers' housing accommodations were improved.[16]

Enlisted men also benefited from Cárdenas' military reforms. In 1935 the first of many Escuelas para Hijos del Ejército was built to provide elementary education for soldiers' children. The following year the first of a series of Military Hospitals was constructed. Enlisted men also received a 10 per cent increase in pay in 1937, and that same year a military life insurance system was established to protect their families. The renovation of old bases and the building of new ones, such as the model Ciudad Militar at Monterrey, brought improved living conditions for the men in the barracks.[17]

Cárdenas provided these material improvements without increasing the army's share of the budget. In fact, the military percentage of the total budget declined under Cárdenas from 25 per cent in 1934 to 19 per cent in 1938.[18]

Cárdenas kept the military expenditures down by placing a 55,000-man ceiling on the army and by closing down marginal facilities. Hidden budgetary benefits were provided by increasing the army's public works activities. For these services, a small payment was made into a Fondo de Trabajo, a kind of savings fund which was delivered to the soldier when he left the service.[19] Still another way in which the President kept military expenses down was by assigning the reserves the local responsibility for preserving internal order. To this end he organized state

119

agrarian contingents which drilled and which were paid only on weekends.[20]

Other economies resulted from organizational changes. In 1935, the previously autonomous Department of Military Factories was brought under the jurisdiction of the War Ministry.[21] The War Ministry itself was reorganized in 1937 and renamed the Ministry of Defense.

Cárdenas was determined to destroy the spirit of caste that the military had developed under Obregón and Calles. In a 1935 address to a graduating class of cadets, Cárdenas declared: "We should not think of ourselves as professional soldiers . . . but rather as armed auxiliaries organized from the humble classes. . . . [Hence,] it is the duty of young officers to broaden the collective spirit of the nation and help incorporate the humble into the whole program of the Revolution." In this same address Cárdenas also announced that a substantial number of the cadets would henceforth be drawn from the enlisted ranks.[22]

Cárdenas also encouraged the enlisted men to become less military and more civilian in spirit. In a series of early 1936 speeches he urged the soldiers to serve the people, to sacrifice themselves to the collective interests of the nation, and to display a democratic comradery with civilians.[23] Two years later he reiterated: "we must reclaim the existence of the military with the daily life of the nation; to the soldier who is isolated in the barracks and living outside society we must reaffirm in him the spirit of a man who continues being a citizen."[24]

The 1939 Law of Obligatory Military Service was another important step in reducing distinctions since it replaced the volunteer system which had often fostered regional militarism. By establishing a lottery that drew equally from all social and economic groups and all regions, more heterogeneous contingents, more *civilista* and nationalistic in spirit, entered the army.[25] In addition to bringing the army closer to the people by making the soldiers more civilian in spirit, Cárdenas also brought the people closer to the army by making civilians more appreciative of the military role. This was largely accomplished through the aforementioned development of agrarian reserves. By the time Cárdenas' term ended in 1940, soldiers were on more intimate terms with civilians than had ever before been the case.

There was a subtle, **BRIDLING THE**   **1936**
yet intimate, relation- **POLITICAL GENERALS**   **1938**
ship between Cár-
denas' Plan Sexenio Militar (to improve the professional quality and material well-being of the armed forces) and his determination to render the revolutionary generals powerless in national politics; and during Cárdenas' presidency, the political power of the revolutionary generals was broken. Those who had heretofore been masters of the state for nearly a quarter century were made servants of the state. Significantly, it required one revolutionary general to break the power of the others.

By 1935, most generals had lost their revolutionary zeal. Too many had become wealthy and, consequently, were opposed to new economic and social reforms. They felt that the radical phase of the Revolution was over; it was time to consolidate; and during this consolidating phase, they expected to continue as the masters of the Mexican nation.

Cárdenas, however, was politically at odds with most of his uniformed colleagues. He believed that now that Mexico had caught its breath under the enforced stability of Calles' regime, it was time to move forward once more—to deepen the Revolution, and to provide benefits to the masses who had hitherto gained very little. Cárdenas was determined to make agrarian reform more meaningful, to distribute more land, and to improve the lot of the peons. He was equally determined to raise the standard of living of organized labor in the urban, mining, and petroleum regions. He also felt an urgent responsibility to raise the educational level of the lower-income groups and to provide them with political rights.

Once Cárdenas subdued the Callista generals, his next problem was to overcome the Cardenista generals. He did it subtly and gradually. His professionalization and modernization program loosened the bonds between the revolutionary generals on the one hand and the junior officers and enlisted men on the other. The *oficiales* were interested in professional military careers. They came to feel that they were better trained—and hence, better qualified to command—than the *divisionarios,* who were politicians rather than soldiers. The lieutenants, captains, and majors clearly viewed Cárdenas as their principal benefactor. Similarly, the enlisted men were fully aware that Cárdenas, rather than their commanders, was the person responsible for improving their lot. Thus in Cárdenas' political struggle with the generals, the men in the ranks and the junior officers became counterpoises for the President.

The agrarian reserves also became a presidential counterpoise to the generals. Made up of peasants, they were under-

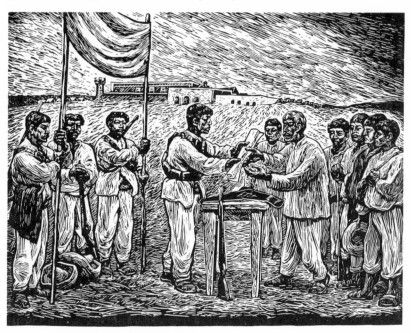

standably enthusiastic about agrarian reform. If the generals wished to block the President's accelerated land redistribution schemes, they would have to consider the prospect of fighting the rural irregulars.[26]

By the end of 1936 the generals were already apprehensive lest the irregulars soon outnumber the regulars. They increasingly complained about the threat of communism. The Gold Shirts had been crushed, but in its place the generals organized the anticommunist National Union of Veterans of the Mexican Revolution.[27] Cárdenas warned this organization in September 1936 that "if conservative elements provoke some crises, the army and the workers will find themselves strongly united in . . . advancing the cause of the Mexican Revolution."[28]

As the President distributed more land to the peasants, encouraged labor to strike for its rights, and raised expenditures for public education and social welfare projects, new cries of alarm were sounded by the military chieftains. On July 13, 1937, the National Union of Veterans of the Mexican Revolution issued a proclmation protesting inflation, labor strikes, and agrarian reform. They charged the government with "disregarding the Constitution and the ideals for which our comrades have laid down their lives."[29] The rising power of the Mexican masses under the Cárdenas administration was clearly feared and resented by most officers who had fought in the Revolution.[30]

But the President was determined not to be throttled by the conservatism of his erstwhile colleagues. To further reduce the generals' political influence and to increase that of the agrarians and organized labor, Cárdenas reorganized the PNR. Since its founding by Calles in 1929, the official party had been an amalgam of local political machines, most of them dominated by the military. But by the end of 1937, Cárdenas began to speak of the need to change the PNR structure so that it would more accurately reflect Mexico's changing political realities. He wanted to replace geographic representation with occupational representation. To this end he proposed that the four main political interest groups—army, labor, agrarians, and popular—be organized into separate party sectors.[31]

In a December 18, 1937, speech, recommending the formation of a military sector for a new official party, Cárdenas stated that he wanted the army officers represented there "not as a deliberating body or as a class corporation which will record an odious doctrine inherent in a special caste, but rather as a citizen reintegration which with collective discipline and high patriotic thoughts and dignity, which is the norm of the army, will continue backing majority opinion and maintaining the integrity of the Constitution and the law."[32]

A month later the President declared: "The present restrictions [against voting] which practically isolate the military from political life . . . are a grave error. . . . Henceforth the members of the army will have, constitutionally, political rights and the duty to exercise them."[33]

The generals were understandably unhappy about the President's proposals, because it was obvious that he was not only forcing their political activities into the open but also diluting their power by bringing labor, peasant, and popular sectors into the decision-making process. On January 31, 1938, Defense Minister General Manuel Avila Camacho announced that the armed forces welcomed the President's call to take part in the formation of a new party. Because this was not true as far as the generals were concerned, he warned them against making any critical statements about the party and insisted that they give the President public support regardless of their private feelings on the matter.[34]

Following orders from Avila Camacho, each zone commander arranged the election of a party representative to the military sector. Ten *brigadieres,* ten *jefes,* and thirteen *oficiales* were selected. In addition, the navy nominated two officers, and the Defense Ministry three. Finally, Avila Camacho appointed two dependable *divisionarios,* Juan José Ríos and Heriberto Jara, to head the military bloc. On March 28, all forty delegates assembled at the Defense Ministry to receive the President's instructions. Two days later they met with the PNR at the Belles Artes Palace. Here the Military Sector dutifully agreed to participate in the new official party as representatives of a "political organization exclusively of a citizen character, and not as representatives of the armed forces, whose military functions will continue absolutely apart from politics."[35]

Thus, on March 30, 1938, the President had his wish as the PNR was convened for the last time, and at the same meeting the Party of the Mexican Revolution (PRM) came into existence. Under its statutes, each of the four sectors was awarded an equal number of party representatives and assigned certain public offices to fill. In any given election, the whole organization would then support the designated sector candidate.[36]

At the time it was organized the PRM claimed nearly four million members, as follows:

Labor Sector	1,250,000
Peasant Sector	2,500,000
Military Sector	55,000
Popular Sector	55,000

It appeared that the military and popular sectors were greatly overrepresented since their forty party representatives each and their six representatives each on the national council of the PRM were equal in number to those of the labor and peasant sectors. The more important consideration, however, was that the army now could be outvoted by the other sectors. When Cárdenas' critics accused him of deliberately bringing the army into politics by putting a military sector in the PRM, he replied: "We did not put the army in politics. It was already there. In fact it had been dominating the situation, and we did well to reduce its influence to one out of four."[37]

Even the "one-out-of-four" reduction does not reveal the full extent of the coup Cárdenas administered to the political generals through the reorganization of the PRM; for the President was able to control the selection of all military delegates through Defense Minister Avila Camacho.[38] Although the latter had fought in the Revolution, he had never risen to senior rank, and was accordingly not considered a *bona fide* revolutionary general. What is more, Cárdenas organized the military sector only on national lines; hence it was unrepresented in the regional party councils, and was thus prevented from intimidating the other sectors at the subnational party levels.[39]

When the PRM was founded, army delegates to the national party convention included only those officers assigned to the military sector. But Cárdenas and Defense Minister Avila Camacho soon encouraged young officers to join the popular, labor and peasant sectors. The army was thus divided into four different political interest groups, and ambitious generals, who might wish to revolt against the rising power of labor and the peasants, had to face the further prospect of possibly fighting against their own officers and men.[40]

One powerful caudillo rebelled, however, less than two months after the PRM was organized. He was General Saturnino Cedillo, who emerged during the violent phase of the Revolution as ruler of the State of San Luis Potosí. Through his use of his private army, he also became one of the nation's largest landowners. Though Cárdenas had allied with Cedillo against Calles and had taken him into the cabinet, the President's campaign to break the political power of the revolutionary generals soon ran counter to Cedillo's vested personal interests. For with Cedillo in the capital, Cárdenas' agents began to infiltrate the San Luis Potosí political machine.[41] In protest Cedillo resigned from the cabinet on August 16, 1937 and returned to San Luis Potosí. When the PRM began organizing here with Cardenista representatives in the spring of 1938, Cedillo rebelled. His private army, however, was no match for the regulars, whom Cárdenas had alerted, and within a few weeks the movement was crushed. Cedillo sought refuge in the mountains, but he was killed in early 1939.

Cedillo had expected other generals, who had also been threatened by Cárdenas' policies, to join his revolt. But he was a man of limited capacity and had little military following outside his own state. Also, many generals still had not fully appreciated the extent to which their political power had been undermined; many naively believed themselves capable of wielding their customary political influence in moments of crisis regardless of the President and the PRM.

Immediately after the founding of **THE ARMY** 1938
the PRM, organized labor became **VERSUS LABOR** 1939
aggressive about rights, privileges, and party offices. Encouraged by the President, trade unions increasingly went on strike to achieve their demands from Mexican and foreign business. On May Day, 1938, a newly organized and uniformed workers' militia, 100,000 strong, paraded en masse through the streets of the capital. Prior to the parade, Cárdenas had warned in a speech that if reactionary forces in the army revolted, they would be obliged to fight these proletarian defenders of his regime.[42]

The revolutionary officers, who still monopolized the upper ranks of the army, were determined to check the political and military rise of organized labor. A conservative congressional bloc, led by generals, attacked the administration's bills designed to strengthen the unions. The revolutionary officers were particularly worried about Lombardo Toledano, Marxist leader of the newly organized Confederación de Trabajadores Mexicanos (CTM). On June 29, 1937 a group of *jefes* issued the following statement: "Lombardo Toledano cannot hide now that he seeks the dissolution of the revolutionary army, and one proof of this is the formation of the so-called workers' militia in order to install a proletarian dictatorship in Mexico. The army is tired of the anti-army calumny by labor leaders like Lombardo who are seeking to fool the workers into starting a fight like that in Spain. The Mexican public may have the secure knowledge that the military officers will put an end to the calumny and violence of perverse leaders who are exploiters of the working class. In good time the army officers will answer their aggressors. We wish it to be known that if our brother officers, in defense of our armed institutions, punish

Lombardo we are not guilty since we have been provoked."[43]
Indeed, army-labor tensions seemed to be moving toward a showdown during the summer of 1938. During June and July, the CTM Council of Sonora demanded the removal of the Governor, General Juan Yocupicio, whom it charged was a dangerous reactionary, "an enemy of the Cárdenas regime," and a Fascist. When General Ramón Iturbe proposed in Congress a democratic front to fight communism, labor and agrarian congressmen tried to expel him. Thereupon, the Association of Revolutionary Patriots came to the defense of General Iturbe.[44]

Military-labor tensions rose to fever pitch in Nuevo León, particularly in the industrial center of Monterrey. When the CTM threatened to strike for broad new material gains and political rights, the Governor, General Anacleto Guerrero, countered with a threat to make Monterrey "the graveyard of the CTM." Governor Guerrero dispatched General Juan Andreu Almazán, Nuevo León's leading industrialist and ranking officer, to the capital to protest the CTM's aggressiveness.[45] Cárdenas, however, ignored the protest.

Troubles of a similar nature plagued Chihuahua and Durango. Military men there discussed measures to stop communism before Lombardo Toledano destroyed the army. Military-labor tensions became so serious in the whole northern tier of states by the fall of 1938 that Cárdenas sent Defense Minister Avila Camacho to investigate and to moderate.[46]

As organized labor began to get the upper hand both in the PRM and in the Cárdenas administration, the revolutionary generals, both active and inactive, became increasingly restive. In October 1938, the Frente Constitucional Democrático, an organization of inactive generals, led by Marcelo Caraveo, Francisco Coss, Pablo González, Fortunato Zuazua, and Jacinto B. Treviño, issued an anti-Communist manifesto. In early December, General Pérez Treviño, who had just resigned from the army in protest against Cárdenas' radical policies, issued an appeal to all Mexicans to join his Anti-Communist Revolutionary Party.[47] Other active anti-labor, anti-Cárdenas associations led by disgruntled military men were the National Union of Veterans of the Revolution and the Nacionalist Vanguard. All of them warned of the threat of communism, and particularly of the communist drive to subvert the army. The government press charged that these "pseudo anti-communist" organizations were reactionary Fascist groups bent on subverting the army zone commanders and overthrowing the Cárdenas government.[48] Regardless of where the truth lay, it was apparent by 1939 that the issue was clearly drawn. Would military conservatives or liberal civilian bureaucrats control the Mexican Revolution? Presumably, that was going to be decided in the 1940 elections.

Sunday July 7, 1940 was the bloodiest **THE 1940 ELECTIONS** election day in the history of the Mexican Revolution. It was the climax of a presidential campaign that had gone on for a year and a half, and it took another half year after the elections to restore political calm. The great issue of the troubled years from 1939 to 1940 was the political future of the hitherto dominant generals of the Mexican Revolution. The significance of the 1940 elections was that these generals, after a severe struggle, were forced to surrender control of Mexico's political processes to civilian politicians. After 1940, no military man ever won the presidency in Mexico again.

By early 1939, three anti-PRM parties, all of them headed by disgruntled generals, were active. The strongest was General Pérez Treviño's Anti-Communist Revolutionary Party (PRAC), a semi-Fascist organization supported by Gold Shirt remnants and Callista generals. Its strength was in the north. The same was true of the Revolutionary Committee of National Reconstruction. This was a rightist organization headed by Carrancista Generals Pablo González and Marcelo Caraveo. Finally, there was General Ramón Iturbe's Constitutional Democratic Front, the only one of the three with significant popular support.[49]

Most public attention was focused upon the PRM, for out of the official party would emerge the likely successor to Cárdenas. The Mexican public got a fair indication of the *presidenciables* on January 17, 1939, when three generals (Defense Minister Manuel Avila Camacho, Communications Minister Francisco Mújica, and First Military Zone Jefe Rafael Sánchez Tapia) took leave from the army—an action required by law for a military man to become candidate for the presidency.[50] One month later, General Joaquín Amaro also took leave.[51]

Mexico's political air was charged with excitement as the military, labor, agrarian and popular sectors of the PRM assembled in the capital on the weekend of February 18-19, 1939, to select the PRM candidate for president. At the same time, the PRAC, in which Villista General Francisco Coss had become prominent, sponsored a Saturday night banquet for all generals of the Revolution and a Sunday afternoon rally for some five thousand veterans of the Revolution.[52]

PRAC favored General Amaro, but it by no means represented the views of the PRM's army sector. The latter quite obviously was controlled by the administration, for the thirty-three zone commanders, whose main qualification for these posts was loyalty to President Cárdenas, had selected the military sector delegates to the PRM. Thus it was no surprise that the military sector cast its vote for General Manuel Avila Camacho. Besides, the Cardenista officers had reason to fear vengeance from the Callistas if General Amaro should win. General Mújica, father of the 1917 Constitution, was too radical to suit most army officers, while Sánchez Tapia was suspect for his clerical associations.

Labor wanted Lombardo Toledano, but he was vetoed by the military and popular sectors. If Cárdenas had tried to impose Lombardo Toledano, he would have encountered the opposition of the entire military organization.[53] Why not General Mújica? Ideologically, he seemed the natural heir to Cárdenas, and as a well-known advocate of land reform and friend of the peons, he had the support of the agrarian sector. Lom-

bardo Toledano and labor, however, were opposed to him, reportedly because Mújica was too close to Trotsky, then in exile in Mexico. Mújica, aware that Cárdenas didn't favor him, warned that the PRM would split into rival camps if the administration attempted to impose a candidate.

Cárdenas didn't have to. Of all those whose hats were in the PRM ring, Avila Camacho was the only one not opposed by at least two of the four sectors. The military sector was already for him, and Cárdenas, concerned over the growing opposition to his radical policies, did not try to block popular sector support for fellow-bureaucrat Avila Camacho. Finally, Lombardo Toledano's personal friendship for Avila Camacho—they had been schoolmates in Puebla in their youth—coupled with his realistic appreciation of what was politically feasible overcame his ideological reservations about the former Defense Minister. When on February 22, 1939, the CTM came out in favor of Avila Camacho, he then had the necessary three sector votes. Later in the year, in early November, he would receive the PRM's official endorsement.[54]

General Avila Camacho, however, was unacceptable to the generals of the Revolution. He was not one of them. He had joined the Constitutionalist Army but had only attained the rank of major by 1920, and his *brigadier* rank was considered a gift from Obregón for his loyalty during the 1923 rebellion. He was not a fighting general; his military reputation had been made in the bureaucracy rather than on the battlefield. He became an executive officer in the War Ministry in 1933, was advanced to Under Secretary in 1934 and to Minister of Defense in 1937. He did not become a *divisionario* until Cárdenas insisted on making him one in 1939. To the revolutionary generals, Avila Camacho was more clerk than soldier.[55] He was unfit, in their eyes, to occupy the presidency, an office which ever since 1920 had been restricted to the fighting generals of the Revolution.

The first to contest Avila Camacho's candidacy was General Joaquín Amaro, acknowledged leader of the Callistas. Chagrined at having received no consideration by the PRM, Amaro readily accepted Pérez Treviño's invitation to head the PRAC ticket. Supporting him were the disgruntled revolutionary generals; businessmen and *hacendados,* alarmed over labor and agrarian aggressiveness, also backed the PRAC, but the Church did not, for Amaro had been associated with Calles' anticlerical policies. Amaro, in March 1939, launched a series of attacks upon the Cárdenas administration, accusing it of excessive agrarianism, demagogic labor policies, maladministration, and communism. His abusiveness was curbed by charging him with complicity in General Serrano's death in 1927 and by threatening him with a trial, confiscation of his extensive properties, and expulsion from the army.[56]

General Sánchez Tapia appealed to the military sector of the PRM, promising the armed forces lavish attention and material benefits should he become president.[57] Failing to get the nomination, he resigned from the PRM and accepted the candidacy of the Constitutional Democratic Front. When he continued to court army support by calling for an expensive new military establishment, the government press condemned his "seditious and unwarranted demagoguery."[58]

About this same time, in the spring of 1939, General Francisco Coss founded the National Party of Public Salvation. Secretary of party organization was General Alfredo Serratos; secretary of military action was General Mariano Flores; and treasurer was Colonel Bernardino Mena Brito. This was a fascist organization. It was anti-Jewish, anti-labor, and anti-United States. It promised to improve the economic lot of the soldiers, to disarm the workers, and "to fulfill its obligations to the veterans of the Revolution."[59] Although the government press used harsh exposure methods on the party, Cárdenas allowed it to function. The National Party of Public Salvation was obviously a crackpot organization, and it soon disintegrated.

Even though the wishes of the four party sectors had been made known in February, some generals sought to win over the PRM leadership before the formal nomination was made in early November. General Mújica continued to campaign until he was certain, in July of 1939, that Cárdenas was going to support Avila Camacho. Thereupon Zapatista General Gilardo Magaña proclaimed himself the fittest to carry on Cárdenas' policies and announced himself a candidate for the PRM nomination. He campaigned ineffectively until just before the PRM's nominating convention, when he also withdrew.[60]

General Juan Andreu Almazán also hoped for the PRM nomination. He became interested once it became clear, in the spring of 1939, that Amaro was not going to be able to make an effective challenge. General Almazán, because he was the highest-ranking officer in the army, felt he had a natural right to the presidency. He expected to receive serious consideration from the PRM, but when the party ignored him, he decided to join the opposition. Encouraged by the revolutionary generals opposed to Avila Camacho, by business and landholder interests opposed to Cárdenas' radical policies, by Morones' Partido Laborista Mexicano, and by certain elements in the Catholic Church, Almazán, on June 30, 1939, resigned his post

133

as commander of the Seventh Military Zone in Monterrey and took leave to campaign for the presidency.[61]

Almazán had joined the Madero revolution in 1910 as a private, but he advanced rapidly as he fought successively for Zapata, Orozco, and Carranza. In 1920 he joined the Agua Prieta rebellion and he became a *divisionario* in 1921. During the 1920's he became director and principal stockholder of the Compañía de Carreteras "Anahuác," a roadbuilding firm, and began investing his profits in industrial and real estate holdings in Monterrey, Mexico City, and Acapulco. He was loyal to President Calles, and as Communications Minister in Ortiz Rubio's cabinet in the early 1930's he enlarged his already considerable fortune by granting government concessions, such as the Pan American highway construction job from Laredo to Mexico City, to the "Anahuác" company. During the Cárdenas administration, he acquired vast holdings in silver mines.[62] By 1939 General Almazán had become one of Mexico's wealthiest citizens.

The various Mexican revolutionary governments had experienced no broadly based political challenge since 1920, but during the latter half of 1939 there began to congregate around Almazán a rather formidable array of outgroups. These consisted of landholders, businessmen, disgruntled labor elements, communists, socialists, and veterans of the Revolution. All of them were somehow assembled under the roof of a single party, the Partido Revolucionario de Unificación Nacional (PRUN). With such a mixture of supporters, Almazán obviously had to be all things to all men, but he was a capable orator, a shrewd campaigner, and soon developed a large popular following.[63]

The Cárdenas administration, in firm control of the election machinery and confident it had a substantial majority, had no real worry that it might lose the election; but it did fear Almazán's military supporters might induce him to lead a rebellion, for thirty-four revolutionary generals took leave to campaign for Almazán. In the event of an uprising, the PRM leaders worried about the attitude of the rest of the army since Almazán had made an open bid for army support by promising wide-spread military reforms that would benefit all officers and men. He also appealed to the veterans of the Revolution, whom he promised to restore to their rightful place in the army.[64]

Cárdenas' apprehension over a military rebellion was reflected in two precautionary measures he took during the summer of 1939. On June 19, General Heriberto Jara, head of the PRM's military sector, replaced lawyer Ruiz Rodríguez as President of the PRM.[65] On September 5, Cárdenas ordered all zone commanders to ban political activity at military installations and instructed all military men to channel their political activity through the military sector of the PRM.[66] In effect, those on active duty were authorized to provide political support for the official candidate only.

But the army did not favor Avila Camacho, and Defence Minister Jesús Augustín Castro had a difficult job keeping the military in line. There was no problem with the high-ranking officers on active duty—the General Staff officers, the zone commanders and the garrison commanders—for they owed their promotions and choice assignments to Cárdenas and Avila Camacho, and, consequently, they were considered little more than political hacks by the Almazanistas. Those below the rank of colonel, however, including the enlisted men, felt that Almazán would do more for the army than Avila Camacho, and they favored the PRUN candidate.[67]

During the early months of 1940, Almazán's campaign greatly increased political tensions. January outbursts of violence in Sonora were attributable to "Almazán's efforts to start a rebellion," charged General Donato Izquierdo, a government spokesman. The following month, speaking in the capital, Almazán said he would indeed start a rebellion "if the government attempts to thwart the will of the people," and he accused Cárdenas of imposing Avila Camacho upon the Mexican people.[68] On May Day, 1940, 30,000 workers demonstrated their support for Avila Camacho by marching through the streets of the capital in military formation. Four days later Lombardo Toledano caused great apprehension in army circles by announcing that the CTM would open its own military college to train officers for the workers militia. This prompted Defense Minister General Augustín Castro to declare that "this ministry considers it opportune to declare that the existence of a militia independent of the only armed force legally authorized in the republic cannot be tolerated."[69]

A month before the election, the zone commanders began to urge support for Avila Camacho. On June 9, for example, General Adrian Castrejón, Jefe de Operaciones in Hidalgo, declared at a rally held for the officers in his zone that "we are going to vote for Avila Camacho because we are identified with the the party of the Revolution and its candidate."[70] Almazán meanwhile reiterated his pledge to lead a rebellion if the government tried to steal the election. The Defense Ministry orders to the zone commanders that the sale or carrying of arms by nonmilitary personnel be suspended for the period July 1-15 suggests that the Cárdenas administration indeed anticipated serious trouble.[71]

On election day, July 7, 1940, there were considerable movements of troops in Mexico's principal cities—troops whose loyalty the Defense Ministry was by no means sure of.[72] Rioting took place at many polling stations and in front of both party headquarters. The casualties in the capital were twenty-seven dead and 152 injured, most of them Almazanistas shot down by armed workers and soldiers.[73]

Six days after the election the government issued the following preliminary results: Avila Camacho, 2,265,199; Almazán, 128,574; Sánchez Tapia, 14,056.[74]

The question now was: could the Cárdenas administration uphold this verdict? During the five months between election day and the inauguration of the new president, it was feared that the PRUN would resort to violence. The PRUN ridiculed the official election figures and claimed a complete victory over the PRM. On July 17, Almazán departed for Havana, promising his followers that the wishes of the Mexican people would be fulfilled.[75]

During August, Almazán repeatedly declared in the United States that he was the victor and that he would "return to Mexico at the opportune moment."[76] In anticipation of this return, PRUN military leaders began planning an uprising; they were apparently convinced that the army, as well as the Mexican people, would back them.[77] Cárdenas clamped down on the PRUN, condemning its activities as "subversive"; he stationed troops around the Chamber of Deputies to bar Almazanistas from trying to take the seats they charged were theirs by default; he praised the army for its proper comportment during the elections. On August 19, the police took General Jacinto B. Treviño into custody for allegedly planning a revolt; they also began strict surveillance over the movements and activities of the other revolutionary generals.[78]

In anticipation of trouble at the September 1, 1940 installation of the new congress, sixty thousand peasants were brought to the capital, and all military leaves were cancelled for the period August 28 to September 3.[79] The new congress was installed on schedule, and Cárdenas, in his last annual message to that body, summed up the achievements of his six years in office. He credited the army with advancing the cause of the Revolution. He defended his policy of bringing the army into politics and, particularly, his grant of the franchise to enlisted men. "As a result of my military policies," he declared, "I am convinced the army has fulfilled its duty in the past and will continue to fulfill it in the future."[80]

Almazán's response to all this was a bitter blast against Cárdenas and an accusation of electoral fraud.[81] Meanwhile, his partisans became impatient for his return, which had been expected at the end of August. On September 13, 1940, Defense Minister Agustín Castro gave the officers who had been granted leaves to campaign for Almazán until October 1 either to return to active service or face charges of desertion.[82]

An Almazanista rump congress met in San Antonio, Texas, and designated General Hector F. López provisional president until Almazán was installed on December 1. As small arms began to be smuggled into northern Mexico, the garrisons were alerted and federal troops set up road blocks and searched all vehicles coming from the United States. On October 7, the government announced it had crushed a conspiracy by two hundred Almazanistas to seize Monterrey. The following day, minor Almazanista disturbances were put down in San Luis Potosí, Durango, Chihuahua, and Puebla.[83]

Following these failures, the revolutionary generals, realizing they had no chance of overthrowing the government, began returning to active duty. The October 1 deadline had passed, but Cárdenas magnanimously took them back into the fold; he even granted them vacations and pay increases in appreciation.[84] By the end of October all the generals who had taken leave to campaign for Almazán had returned to active duty. On November 16, the Almazanista rump congress disbanded in San Antonio.[85]

Almazán's followers felt let down since he did not return as promised. Quite naturally, Almazán was unwilling to risk confiscation of his huge personal holdings in Mexico should a revolt fail. Success depended on a sympathetic response to his cause in the United States, which would insure that arms would be forthcoming. But he did not get the desired assurance, and so he gave up. General Almazán returned to Mexico at the end of November, not to lead a revolt but to attend Avila Camacho's inauguration. Cárdenas thereupon invited him to return to active duty.[86]

The last threat to the government by the generals of the Revolution had been eliminated. On December 1, 1940, Avila Camacho was inaugurated President of Mexico.

VI

EPILOGUE

The significance of the 1940 elections in reducing the political influence of the military becomes fully apparent when the subsequent quarter century is examined. With decision-making power in the hands of civilians, the relative importance of the military declined with each passing year. The most striking effect of civilian political control has been the progressive reduction of the percentage of the national budget allotted to the armed forces.

Defense figures include only the army and the air force expenditures, but during the early 1940's Mexico also began to develop a navy. This appropriation, which also included the merchant marine, was included in the Marine Ministry. The figures have varied over the years, but around half the Marine Ministry's appropriation has been for the navy. The Marine budget has been from 2 to 4 per cent of the total budget over the past generation, and during the 1960's has remained stable

MILITARY BUDGETS, 1940-1966[1]
(figures in millions of pesos)

year	total budget	defense budget	defense budget as % of total
1940	449	94	21
1941	493	110	22
1942	555	120	22
1943	707	147	21
1944	1102	160	14
1945	1007	170	15
1946	1201	182	15
1947	1667	220	13
1948	2303	240	10
1949	2551	262	10
1950	2746	262	10
1951	3103	275	10
1952	3999	329	8
1953	4160	370	9
1954	4827	409	8
1955	5681	409	8
1956	6696	507	7
1957	7567	557	7
1958	8402	591	7
1959	9386	663	7
1960	10256	752	7
1961	11041	760	7
1962	12320	822	7
1963	13801	958	7
1964	15953	1062	7
1965	17854	1232	7
1966	20132	1333	7

at 3 per cent. Since 1½ per cent of this is for the navy, Mexico's combined armed forces expenditure then amounts to about 8½ per cent of the total, a percentage which has remained fixed over the past decade.

Although there have been constantly rising military expenditures over the past quarter century, these have not been nearly so pronounced as the figures would seem to indicate. Adjusting for a seven-fold increase in the price index (from 34 in 1940 to 240 in 1966), the real military budget has increased only 88 per cent over the past quarter century whereas the real total budget has risen 617 per cent during this same period. The relative decline in military spending is equally revealing when adjustments are made for population growth. Whereas real per capita military expenditures have remained virtually constant over the past quarter century (at about 15 pesos per capita in 1950 constant pesos) real per capita overall government expenditures have nearly trebled.[2]

Under the presidency of Manuel Avila Camacho (1940-1946), the influence of the military was greatly reduced because middle class civilian control of Mexico's politics was finally consolidated. Soon after his inauguration, Avila Camacho eliminated the military sector from the official party. Thereupon, most officers left the party; those who remained joined the popular sector.[3] During 1941 the military bloc in Congress was broken down and its members were absorbed into the various class, occupational, and regional groupings inside that body. The President meanwhile retired a number of revolutionary generals because they lacked the technical qualifications required for the modern warfare methods being used in World War II.[4] The only generals in Avila Camacho's cabinet were Marine Minister Heriberto Jara, Defense Minister Lázaro Cárdenas (the man still most capable of keeping the army under control), and Communications and Public Works Minister Maximino Avila Camacho, the President's brother.

Avila Camacho used the emergency of World War II to insist that the army devote itself exclusively to military functions, especially the defense of Mexico against possible foreign attack. To help modernize the military establishment, he welcomed United States assistance. In exchange, Mexico provided a token cooperation to hemispheric defense, permitting U.S.

143

military overflights and contributing an air force fighter squadron to the Allied Forces in the Pacific.[5] Though the Mexican government expressed great concern for defense in World War II, no expansion of its armed forces occurred. In fact, between the years 1941 and 1944, Avila Camacho pared Defense's share of the budget from 22 per cent to 14.

As soon as World War II ended the President began implementing the 1936 retirement law under which the career span for officers was reduced from thirty-five years to twenty-five; 550 of Mexico's revolutionary generals and an equal number of colonels were forced into retirement. Avila Camacho took this action not only to rid the army of technically unqualified generals and colonels but also to make it possible for academy-trained officers to be promoted. He explained that the retirements would assist in "completing the transformation of the Army from what was once regarded as a political factor into a nonpolitical and purely professional corps at the service of the State."[6] Protests from the generals—that "technical qualification" was a sham issue, that it was unjust to retire those who so long served the cause of the nation and the Revolution, and that they were not as old as many generals in the United States and Western Europe—were fruitless.[7]

In 1945, when the PRM was reorganized and renamed the Institutional Revolutionary Party (PRI) no military candidate emerged to challenge lawyer Miguel Alemán. And in the 1946 elections, since the generals were without a presidential contender, they had to voice their opposition to the government through the Party of National Action (PAN) ticket, headed by Ezekiel Padilla.

President Miguel Alemán (1946-1952) continued to undermine both the political influence and institutional importance of the military. Under his administration the Defense Ministry's share of the budget was reduced from 15 per cent in 1946 to 8 per cent in 1952. Such reductions demonstrated that civilians were now making the decisions with respect to the size and character of the military organization.

The supremacy of Mexico's civilian authorities was clearly displayed at the Ninth International Conference of American States when this body met in Bogotá in the spring of 1948. Here the Charter of the Organization of American States was framed. The proposal in the draft charter for a defense council to deal with military matters was omitted solely because of Mexico's objection. Mexico's military advisers to the conference were in full agreement with their uniformed colleagues from the rest of Latin America and the United States that a defense council should be set up under the OAS, but they were overruled by their civilian foreign minister.[8]

Four years later, the Alemán administration again overruled the military on a hemisphere defense matter. Late in 1951, the United States began negotiations with eight Latin-American countries for military defense assistance pacts, under which the countries involved were to receive military assistance from the United States in exchange for agreeing to assume certain hemisphere defense responsibilities. All the countries approached, save Mexico, signed such pacts. Mexico's military men desired such an agreement in order to get new military equipment, but they were overruled by the civilian authorities.[9]

The final political defeat of generals of the Revolution came in the presidential elections of 1952. In the spring of that year General Vejar Vásquez, defying regulations prohibiting officers on the active duty lists from engaging in politics, accepted the presidency of Vicente Lombardo Toledano's Popular Party and began to urge formation of a coalition to fight the PRI. For his efforts he was arrested and tried before a military court. His protests that General Rodolfo Sánchez, President of the PRI, and General Alfonso Corona del Rosal, head of the PRI's regional committee in Mexico City, were active in politics, availed him nothing.[10] Ultimately, General Miguel Henríquez Guzmán, a millionaire contractor, became the candidate of the dissident Federation of People's Parties (FPP). He had been disappointed when the PRI ignored him in favor of Alemán in 1946 and was doubly disappointed when the PRI bypassed him again in 1952, this time in favor of Adolfo Ruiz Cortines, Alemán's civilian Minister of Government. Some old generals of the Revolution and members of the Veterans of the Revolution supported General Henríquez, and there was talk of revolt, but nothing as serious as in 1940. The regular army maintained a discreet and silent apolitical stance as Ruiz Cortines garnered over three-fourth of the popular vote.

The Ruiz Cortines administration was one of firm and continuing civilian supremacy over the military. While the rest of the government apparatus expanded, the armed forces were kept at fifty thousand, and their share of the budget was reduced to 7 per cent. By the time of the 1958 elections there were simply no more revolutionary generals left who could be considered serious presidential candidates. They had either died or simply disappeared from public life. For the first time, no uniformed presidential hopeful appeared inside the ranks of the official party. Even the PAN was obligated to nominate a civilian candidate. PRI candidate Adolfo López Mateos, Labor Minister under Ruiz Cortines, won the presidency with over 90 per cent of the vote and served out his six year term, uncomplicated by any resistance from the military. He was succeeded by another civilian bureaucrat, Gustavo Díaz Ordaz, at the end of 1964.

MEXICO TODAY is one of the most lightly armed nations in the world. Only one out of every eight hundred citizens is in uniform. The 50,000-man military establishment is the same size today as it was a quarter of a century ago, even though the population has doubled from twenty million to forty million since 1940. The 1966 budget for the army and air forces amounted to a modest 1333 million pesos ($107 million), or just under 7 per cent of the total budget. Combat forces in the navy got 300 million ($22 million), or about 1½ per cent of the total. Thus the composite armed forces budget was about one-twelfth of the total, a relatively small fraction compared to nations like Brazil and Argentina, for example, where the military receives nearly one-sixth of the total. Also contributing to the

146

modest military budget in Mexico is a minimum expenditure upon equipment. Military hardware is purchased neither for display nor for defense against a quite improbable external threat, but only for purposes of preserving internal order.

Heading the defense establishment is General Marcelino García Barragán. An enlisted man in the violent phase of the Revolution, he attended the military academy under Carranza's presidency and became an officer upon graduation in 1920. He established a reputation as a bright young professional officer, worked his way up through the various grades to brigadier general, and became Director of the Military Academy in 1941. He also served as governor of his home State of Jalisco in 1943. He is a representative of the academy-trained professionals who began to run the Mexican Army after World War II. Today there are very few of the old generals of the Revolution left, and the small number still on active duty do not have positions of influence. The Veterans of the Revolution are no longer taken seriously by either the political or military authorities.

There are just under four thousand officers, about one for every twelve enlisted men. The cadets who gain entry to the Colegio Militar (about 250 annually) and the Escuela Militar de Aviación (about 50 annually) come mainly from middle-class families. A competitive entry examination and a 500-peso admission fee screen out the uneducated and the poor. The young men plan their professional careers carefully and obtain promotions through professional competence rather than through political influence as in the past. A young officer's pay obliges him to lead a semi-spartan life during the early years of his career, but he can look forward to a fairly comfortable middle-class existence once he reaches the rank of colonel. At that time, the more promising ones who can be expected to be promoted to generals will be sent to the Escuela Superior de Guerra, where they will be trained for staff duty. Some are sent for advanced training to military schools in the United States.

In contrast to the officer corps, the enlisted ranks are made up of short term (one to three years) conscripts and volunteers.

Mexico has conscription today, but a modest amount of wealth, influence, or education is generally enough to avoid serving. Most of those reporting for military service are rural folk, and a fairly high percentage of these are illiterate. For such draftees army life represents an education as well as an improvement in their customary standard of living.

The army is divided into ten military regions and thirty-four command zones, in which are found infantry, cavalry, artillery, and engineering detachments. There is also an elite presidential guard of four thousand.

The air force is a branch of the army, and only one-tenth as large. There are ten air squadrons, a special paratroop battalion, and several air force training schools. The combat navy is also small (about 4500) and its principal training schools and base facilities are in Veracruz. Naval vessels consist mainly of frigates and coastal patrol craft.[11]

Although military men have been denied the presidency for over a generation, they have been given the top post in the PRI. But this post is not awarded to the most powerful and influential military man. President of the PRI between 1952 and 1964 was General and Licenciado Alfonso Corona del Rosal, a man more widely recognized for his legal prestige than his military prowess. Besides, the President of Mexico is the real power in the PRI, and the PRI president is merely his agent. Although about a quarter of the twenty gubernatorial posts and a tenth of the 238 congressional seats are now filled by military men, their selection cannot be attributed to pressures exerted by the military as a political interest group. Rather, these gubernatorial and congressional political posts go to certain military men because of personal followings they still enjoy in their home states or congressional districts.

The political role of the army has all but disappeared, and the reason this has occurred is not only because the civilian element has become supreme, but also because the army has lost the social mission it had during the first quarter century of the Revolution. Today it has become a pliable and disciplined tool

148

of the civilian leaders of the Mexican nation.[12] Jean Juarès' nineteenth-century description of the French army would equally well fit the Mexican army of today: "The army is but an instrument. It has neither strength of its own, nor an independent will, nor an individual policy." There is a kind of gentleman's agreement between the civilian and military authorities whereby it is understood that army officers will be provided reasonable living standards. For these economic rewards the armed forces are expected to remain loyal to the PRI. The armed forces feel they are performing a necessary and legitimate military function. To continue performing it, they need a minimum level of financial support. When, under Ruiz Cortines, the defense budget dropped to 7 per cent, living conditions, equipment, training facilities, and opportunities for advancement were considered something less than adequate for those in the junior-officer ranks. Despite some grumbling, resentment, and restlessness, it remains at 7 per cent today.

Still, Mexico's officers have a marked esprit de corps. They are not concerned with political power itself, but they are concerned lest civilian politicians deny officers their just due. They want to be recognized as having a vital role in preserving internal order and defending Mexico's sovereignty. They want their profession respected by both the people and the government. Their social and political mentality is middle class. Though continuing to masquerade as guardians of the Mexican Revolution, they dislike extremists of the left as well as the right. They have little concern for the aspirations of lower-income groups. Mexico's moderate, middle-of-the-road governments of the past quarter century have been in tune with the social philosophy of the officer class. This is an added reason why militarism has been no problem in Mexico since 1940.

The civilian authorities do not agree with the military's image of itself. They feel that the military has no vital role in defending the nation against an external threat, for there is no such threat. Accordingly, they have reduced military budgets, equipment expenditures, and force levels to a minimum necessary for maintaining internal order. An officer's career is less prestigious than most other professional occupations. The pay is lower, and the quality of a man who chooses a military career is considered somewhat limited. Generally speaking, civilian professional groups consider military professionals unqualified for political office and nonmilitary administration.

The ruling middle-class element, though it has a rather low estimate of the military, needs and uses it to enhance its own position. Extreme leftists, unhappy with what they consider the overly conservative tone of the government, see the army as an impediment to rapid social change and social reform and would like to see it dispersed. Forces on the extreme right, however, would probably like to undermine it and use it against the middle class that rules Mexico today.

The likelihood that the Mexican military can be swayed from its professional apolitical behavior in the foreseeable future seems remote indeed. Overt manifestation of a junior officer's professional discontent means the abrupt end of his career. Senior officers are reasonably happy with the emoluments and privileges they receive under the present system.

The factor that has created such extraordinary political stability in Mexico and, accordingly, such a small degree of restlessness in the armed forces, is the broad consensus of popular support enjoyed by the ruling PRI and the central government. The great danger for the future, of course, is that the consensus may begin to break down. In this event, the resurgence of the military in politics would seem probable, if for no other reason than that no government in Mexican history has ever surrendered as a result of an electoral defeat, and thus the only way an opposition majority could achieve power would be by force.

This would not guarantee that the armed forces would emerge as political arbiters. Rather, they could only be participants. For the Mexican military institution is small and weak. There are few Mexicans in the regular army, and the latter by no means has a monopoly on the means of violence. The agrarian irregulars, which drill each weekend, are larger than the regulars, and the police, as well as future guerrilla forces, could prove effective counterpoises. So, regardless of the presence or absence of continued political stability in Mexico, the armed forces in that nation, unless they become enlarged considerably, would appear to have little or no political future.

APPENDIX A

PROJECTED MILITARY BUDGETS, 1914-1940*

(figures in millions of pesos)

year	total budget	military budget **	military % of total
1914	141	44	31
1915	140	43	31
1916***			
1917	177	127	72
1918	187	120	64
1919	203	134	66
1920	213	132	65
1921	251	153	61
1922	384	166	41
1923	348	126	36
1924	298	108	36
1925	304	95	31
1926	304	95	31
1927	319	90	25
1928	291	97	33
1929	288	98	34
1930	294	93	32
1931	300	80	27
1932	227	61	27
1933	245	61	25
1934	243	61	25
1935	275	62	23
1936	287	70	24
1937	333	80	24
1938	431	84	19
1939	445	93	21
1940	449	94	21

* Source: Secretaría de Hacienda, *Memoria y Cuenta*, 1914-1940.
** Figure includes Defense Ministry appropriation plus those for the Military Factories.   *** No reliable figures available.

APPENDIX B

GOVERNORS AS OF JULY 11, 1918

Agua Calientes—Civilian
Lower California—Colonel Esteben Cantú (elected)
Coahuila—Civilian
Chihuahua—General Ignacio C. Enríquez (not elected)
Chiapas—Colonel Pablo Villanueva (not elected)
Durango—Civilian
Federal District—General Alfredo Briceida (appointed by president)
Guanajuato—Civilian
Guerrero—Civilian (Gen. Silvestre Marical had been elected governor here but was put in jail for treason).
Hildalgo—General Nicolás Flores (elected)
Jalisco—General Manuel Diéguez (elected)
México—General Agustín Castro (elected)
Morelos—(no governor here since Zapatistas were dominant)
Michoacán—General Pasqual Ortíz Rubio (elected)
Nueva León—Civilian
Nayarit—General Juan José Camarena (not elected)
Oaxaca—General Juan Jiménez (not elected)
Puebla—Civilian
Quintana Roo—Colonel Faustino Lamarage (not elected)
Querétaro—Civilian
Sonora—General Plutarco Elías Calles (elected)
Sinaloa—General Ramón F. Iturbi (elected)
San Luis Potosí—General Juan Barragán (elected)
Tabasco—General Luis G. Hernández (not elected)
Tlaxcala—Civilian
Tamaulipas—Civilian
Veracruz—General Cándido Aguilar (elected)
Yucatán—General Carlos Castro (not elected)
Zacatecas—Civilian

APPENDIX C

MILITARY DELEGATES: QUERÉTARO CONVENTION

Left
Gen. Francisco Mújica
Gen. Cándido Aguilar
Gen. Amado
Col. Alvaro L. Allende
Col. José Ancona Albertos
Gen. Gabino Barrera
Lt. Col. Antonio de la Bojórquez
Col. Donato Calderón
Gen. Esteban Baca Canio
Lt. Col. Galdino H. Castillo
Col. Porfirio del Cedano
Maj. Marcelino Cervantes
Col. Eliseo L. Colunga
Lt. Col. Federico Dyer
Maj. Luis Esquerro
Col. Adolfo G. García
Col. Emiliano C. Garza Zambranio
Col. José L. Góngora
Maj. Modesto González Torres
Gen. Salvador Gracidas
Gen. Heriberto Jara
Gen. Francisco Labastida

Izquierdo
Lt. Col. Cristóbal Lopéz Guerra
Col. José Márquez Rafael

Gen. Francisco J. Navarro
Col. Luis T. Ocampo
Col. Benito Ramírez Llaca
Maj. José Robledo
Col. Matías Raél
Col. Gabriel Román
Lt. Col. José P. Ruiz
Lt. Col. Leopoldo Sánchez
Col. Ascensión Terrones B.

Right
Gen. Martín Cepeda Medrano
Col. Gabriel R. Cravioto
Col. Pedro A. Dávalos
Col. Gilberto de la Garza González
Gen. Reynaldo Gómez Palacio
Col. Epigmenio A. Martínez
Mendoza
Gen. Emiliano P. Navarro
Col. Gilberto M. Ochoa
Gen. Ignacio L. Prieto
Gen. José Ma. Rojas
Gen. Samuel de los Sepúlveda

Uncommitted
Gen. Francisco Lopéz Couto

NOTES

NOTES TO CHAPTER ONE

1 Carlton Beals, *Porfirio Díaz* (Philadelphia, Lippincott, 1932), pp. 222-255.

2 Beals, pp. 222-255; Stanley R. Ross, *Francisco I. Madero: Apostle of Mexican Democracy* (New York, Columbia University Press, 1955), p. 24.

3 Manuel González Ramírez, *Planes políticos y otros documentos* (Mexico, D.F., 1954), p. xii; Beals, pp. 223-224.

4 Ross, p. 25.

5 Ernest Gruening, *Mexico and its Heritage* (New York, Appleton-Century, 1928), pp. 301-302.

6 Thomas A. Janvier, "The Mexican Army," in *The Armies of Today* (New York, 1893), pp. 366-396; Charles M. Jerram, *Armies of the World* (London, 1899), pp. 206-207, 299.

7 Jerram, pp. 206-207, 299.

8 *Mexico in the Twentieth Century* (London, L. E. Arnold, 1907), II, 42-43.

9 Janvier, pp. 370-374.

10 Jerram, p. 206. The United States army at this time had the same number of enlisted men as Mexico but less than one-fourth as many officers.

11 William P. Tucker, *The Mexican Government Today* (Minneapolis, University of Minnesota Press, 1957), pp. 192-193.

12 General Cristobal Rodríguez, "El ejército de ayer," in *La Patria,* 18 Dec. 1926.

13 Alfonso Corona del Rosal, "El ejército y la revolución mexicana," in *El Popular,* July 1, 1938.

14 For social background on prominent men of the Mexican Revolution see Daniel Moreno, *Los hombres de la revolución,* (Mexico, D. F., 1960).

15 Juan Barragán Rodríguez, *Historia del ejército y de la Revolución Constitutionalista* (2 vols., Mexico, D. F., 1946) , I: 248.

16 *The Natural History of Revolution* (Chicago, Univ. of Chicago Press, 1927), p. 7.

17 Francisco I. Madero, *La sucesión presidencial en 1910* (Paris, C. Bouret, 1908), pp. 28-81.

18 Madero, pp. 63-64. Madero's campaign against militarism stole the thunder of Flores Magón's Liberal party. The latter's revolutionary plan of July 1, 1906, issued from St. Louis, called "for suppression of obligatory military service" and for "all military tribunals to be suppressed." See Articles 5 and 9 of the "plan" in Francisco Naranjo, *Diccionario biográfico revolucionario* (Mexico, D.F., 1935), p. 358.

19 Madero to Pino Suárez, April 16, 1910, Archivo de Madero, cited in Ross, p. 100.

20 Articles 2 and 7 of the Plan of San Luis Potosí, Oct. 5, 1910, in Naranjo, pp. 264-270.

21 Transitory provisions, Naranjo, pp. 267-268.

22 Manuel González Ramírez, *La revolución social de México* (Mexico, D.F., 1960) , pp. 274-275.

23 Article 8, in Naranjo, p. 270.

24 Alfonso Terracena, *Mi vida en el vertigo de la revolución mejicana* (Mexico, D.F., 1936) , pp. 342-345.

25 Ross, pp. 121-143.

26 Monica Nash, "El ejército: los ascensos," in *Diario Sureste,* July 11, 1937.

27 Charles Cumberland, *The Mexican Revolution: Genesis under Madero* (Austin, Univ. of Texas Press, 1952), pp. 144-145.

28 U.S. Military Attache Captain Gerard Sturdevant to War Department, Mexico, D.F., April 19, 1911, Archives of the United States Department of State (ADS), 812.00/1360.

29 Jesus Silva Herzog maintains that "the triumph of the Madero revolution was not due to arms but to the pressure of public opinion."

See his *Un ensayo sobre la revolución mejicana* (Mexico, D.F., 1946), pp. 128-129.

30 Jorge Vera Estañol, *La revolución mejicana: orígenes y resultados* (Mexico, D.F., 1957), pp. 48-50; Sturdevant to War Department, Mexico, D.F., April 1, 1911, ADS, 812.22/1.

31 Vera Estañol, pp. 50-51.

32 Vera Estañol, pp. 51-53; Sturdevant to War Department, Mexico, D.F., April 1, 1911, ADS 812.aa/1; Ambassador Henry Lane Wilson to Secretary of State, Mexico, D.F., February 6, 1911. When riots broke out in the capital, the army was able to come up with only two functioning machine guns for quelling the popular disturbances.

33 Gruening, p. 302.

34 Vera Estañol, p. 53.

35 Ross, p. 170.

36 González Ramírez, *La revolución social,* pp. 274-275.

37 Rosendo Salazar, *Del militarismo al civilismo en México* (Mexico, D.F., 1936), p. 153.

38 Walter Fornaro, *Carranza and Mexico* (New York, M. Kennerly, 1915), pp. 15-16.

39 Francisco Vásquez Gómez, *Memorias políticas* (Mexico D.F., 1933), p. 306.

40 *El Imparcial,* June 30, 1911.

41 Chargé Dearing to Sec. of State, Mexico, D.F., Aug. 4, 1911, ADS 812.00/2257.

42 González Ramírez, *La revolución social,* p. 243.

43 Ross, pp. 178-80.

44 Chargé Dearing to Sec. of State, Mexico, D.F., Dispatches of Aug. 23, 26 and Sept. 4, 1911, ADS 812.00/2304, 2318 and 2344.

45 Cumberland, p. 248.

46 Articles 3 and 10 of Plan of Ayala in Naranjo, pp. 272-274.

47 Wilson to Secretary of State, Mexico, D.F., Dispatches of Dec. 6 and 18, 1911, ADS 812.00/2599 and 2635; Ross, pp. 254-255.

48 See his *Mexican Rebel: Pascual Orozco and the Mexican Revolution, 1910-1915* (Lincoln, University of Nebraska Press, 1967).

49 Wilson to Secretary of State, Mexico, D.F., Dispatches of March 17, 19, May 1, 21, 1912, ADS 812.00/3300, 3262, 3770, 3970; Consul Thomas D. Edwards to Secretary of State, Ciudad Juárez, February 1, 1912, ADS 812.00/2717.

50 Cumberland, pp. 190-205; Ross, pp. 256-267.

51 Plan Felicista, Vera Cruz, Oct. 16, 1912, in Naranjo, pp. 284-285. González Ramírez observed that the Plan Felicista merely masked an "ambition to become president and to restore a Díaz-type regime." See his *Planes poltíticos,* p. xlix.

52 Hamm to Sec. of State, Mexico, D.F., Oct. 19, 1912, ADS 812.00/5283; Schuyler to Sec. of State, Mexico, D.F., Oct. 21, 1912, ADS 812.00/5306.

53 Just prior to the coup, the U.S. Embassy reported a notable rise in public disorders. The author has been unable to substantiate this from Mexican sources. See Wilson to Sec. of State, Mexico, D.F., Dispatches of Jan. 7, 31, Feb. 14, 1913, ADS 812.00/5823, 5983, 6068.

54 See Ross, pp. 280-304 and Cumberland, pp. 232-240.

55 González Ramírez, *La revolución social,* pp. 244-246.

56 Barrigán, I: 618.

57 Cumberland, p. 256.

58 ADS, 812.00/7933 and 10,077.

59 For a revisionist view of the old Huerta image see Richard Greenleaf and William Sherman, *Victoriano Huerta: a Reappraisal* (Mexico, D.F., 1960).

60 González Ramírez, *La revolución social,* pp. 239-240.

61 Dispatch to Sec. of State, Vera Cruz, Nov. 18, 1913, ADS 812.00/9812.

62 Gen. J. (Anónimo), "La reorganización del ejército," in *El Universal,* May 7, 1925.

63 Capt. W. Burnside to War Dept., Mexico, D.F., April 30, 1913, ADS 812.00/7575.

64 Juan de Dios Bojórquez, *Obregón, apuntes biográficas* (Mexico, D.F., 1929), pp. 16-17.

65 Barragán, I: 219-226.

66 Salazar, p. 233.

67 Barragán, I: 163-165.

68 Barragán, I: 161, 205, 268-289, 607-610. War telegrams from these generals in the Defense Archives show they were all literate.

69 Obregón's military career began in 1912 when he led volunteers, in behalf of the Madero government, against Orozco.

70 Ross, p. 340.

71 Barragán, I: 79-88. Carranza, who had been Secretary of War briefly under Madero, invited the Federal generals, unsuccessfully, to defect to his movement.

72 Salazar, pp. 231-233.

73 González, Ramírez, *La revolución social*, pp. 247-248.

74 Articles 1-6, Plan of Guadaloupe in Naranjo, pp. 287-288.

75 Barragán's two volume work is still the best military history of the Constitutionalist Revolution. But see also, Obregón's *Ocho mil kilometros en campaña* (Paris, C. Bouret, 1917).

76 Barragán, I: 116-118, 244-245; Robert Quirk, *The Mexican Revolution, 1914-1915; the Convention of Aquascalientes* (Bloomington, Indiana Univ. Press. 1960), pp. 10-11.

77 Barragán, I: 593-605; Quirk, pp. 45-60.

NOTES TO CHAPTER TWO

1 Vera Estañol, pp. 386-387.

2 *El Liberal*, Oct. 5, 1914.

3 Luis Mendieta y Nuñez, "Los civiles de la revolución," in *El Universal*, May 9, 1945.

4 Obviously, this was in direct violation of the Treaty of Teoloyucan. Barragán, II: 29, 54-55.

5 The finest piece of scholarship on the Aguascalientes Convention is Robert Quirk's *Mexican Revolution, 1914-1915*. See pp. 61-86 for background to the convention.

6 Quoted in Quirk, p. 95.

7 Quirk, p. 126.

8 Barragán, I: 172, 217.

9 Quoted in Quirk, p. 196.

10 Alberto J. Pani, "El cambio de regimes en México y los asesinatos millitares," in *El Universal*, January 1, 1930.

11 Estimate of Headquarters, Fort Sam Houston, Texas, to War Department, Nov. 9, 1914, ADS 8, 812.00/13718.

12 U.S. Consul Cobb, El Paso, to Sec. of State, El Paso, ADS 812.00/17571.

13 Barragán, I: 503-508, II: 53-54.

14 Quirk, pp. 126-179.

15 The best study of this episode is Clarence C. Clenendon, *The United States and Pancho Villa* (Ithaca, Cornell Univ. Press, 1961).

16 U.S. Consul Parker to Sec. of State, Querétaro, Jan. 10, 1917, ADS 812.00/20433.

17 Summerlin to Sec. of State, Mexico, D.F., Jan. 9, 1918, ADS 812.00/21660.

18 Map and publication accompanying Dispatch to Sec. of State, Nov. 16, 1919, Mexico, D.F., ADS 812.00/23370.

19 Broadside issued by the National Reorganization Army of Mexico. Felix Díaz's conspiracies, backed by rightist civilian elements, continued into the 1920's.

20 General Rubén García, "El Ejército Nacional" in *El Legionario*, August, 1946, pp. 55-56; Funston to Sec. of State, Vera Cruz, Aug. 15, 1914, ADS 812.00/12883.

21 Emilio Portes Gil, *Quince años de política mexicana* (Mexico, D.F., 1941), pp. 232-237.

22 Editorial, "Cabrera sigue defendienda la indefensible," in *El Heraldo de Mexico*, June 6, 1920.

23 See appendix B.

24 Portes Gil, pp. 237-238.

25 Ingraham, Asst. Sec. of War to Sec. of State, Washington, Sept. 18, 1916, ADS 812.00/19295.

26 Parker to Sec. of State, Querétaro, Jan. 10, 1917, ADS 812.00/20433.

27 U.S. Consul J. B. Stewart to Sec. of State, Chihuahua, Oct. 12, 1918, ADS 812.00/22331. For this insubordination, General Murguía was reprimanded. He was retired temporarily from active service and replaced by General Agustín Castro as Jefe de Operaciones Militares in Chihuahua. See Fletcher to Sec. of State, Mexico, D.F., Nov. 26, 1918, ADS 812.00/22389.

28 Summerlin to Sec. of State, Mexico, D.F., April 22, 1919, ADS 812.00/22663.

29 Vicente Blasco Ibañez, *El militarismo mejicano* (Valencia, Prometeo, 1920), pp. 179, 184.

30 Cited in Daniels, Sec. Navy to Sec. of State, Washington, June 27, 1914, ADS 812.00/12197.

31 Barragán, II: 297.

32 Quirk, pp. 144-145.

33 Major Campbell, Mil. Attache, to Mil. Intelligence, Mexico, D.F., July 1, 1918, ADS 812.00/22110.

34 John W. F. Dulles, *Yesterday in Mexico* (Austin, Univ. of Texas Press, 1961), p. 72. The following year, General Guajardo was one of the first to turn traitor to Carranza.

35 Consular Agent Charles Arthur to Embassy, Oaxaca, Oct. 18, 1918, ADS 812.00/22436.

36 Consul Claude Dawson to Sec. of State, Tampico, June 29, 1918, ADS 812.00/22098.

37 Summerlin to Sec. of State, Mexico, D.F., Sept. 9, 1919, ADS 812.20/17.

38 Blasco Ibañez, pp. 105, 108-112; Vera Estañol, pp. 490-492. González, like Guajardo, did not hesitate to defect from Carranza at the first opportune moment.

39 Gruening, p. 318.

40 Carothers to Sec. of State, Chihuahua, Sept. 13, 1916, ADS 812.00/19204; Stewart to Sec. of State, Chihuahua, Aug. 15, 1919, ADS 812.00/22978.

41 Jan. 10, 1917, dispatch to Sec. of State, ADS 812.00/20433.

42 Chamberlain to Sec. of State, Mexico, D.F., Jan. 31, 1919, and Hanna to Sec. of State, San Antonio, Dec. 26, 1918. ADS 812.00/22509 and 22440.

43 Blasco Ibañez, p. 179.

44 Parker to Sec. of State, Mexico, D.F., Oct. 24, 1916, ADS 812.00/19632.

45 "El Congreso Constituyente de Querétaro," *Gráfico* (Magazín del Gráfico), Feb. 7, 1932.

46 González Ramírez, *Planes politicos,* pp. xlvi-xlvii.

47 Parker to Sec. of State, Querétaro, Dec. 6, 1916, ADS 812.00/20033. Cándido Aguilar was the only *divisionario* delegate to the convention.

48 Thurston to Sec. of State, Mexico, D.F., Dec. 22, 1916, ADS 812.00/20140.

49 Parker, to Sec. of State, Querétaro Jan. 11, 1917, ADS 812.00/20258.

50 For a list of military delegates at the Querétaro Convention see appendix C.

51 Anónima, "Obregón en el Constituyente," in *El Nacional*, July 17, 1943; Bojórquez, p. 41; Santiago Piño Soria, "Nuestra ejército: guardian de la institucionalidad," in *El Nacional*, Nov. 20, 1941. See articles 3, 27, 123 and 130 in the 1917 Constitution.

52 See Antonio Ancona Albertos' "El ejército y el congreso constituyente" speech before the Commission on Military Studies, reprinted in *El Nacional,* Feb. 8, 1936.

53 See Eduardo Palleres, "Antimilitarismo constitucional," in *El Universal,* May 25, 1945.

54 Constitutional reform of Feb. 22, 1927.

55 José Espejel Flores, "Antecedentes de interpretación del artículo 13 constitucional," in *Boletín Jurídico Militar,* July- Sept. 1954, pp. 180-186.

56 Juan de Dios Bojórquez, *Crónica del constituyente* (Mexico, D.F., 1938), pp. 255-264. This book and Felix Palavacini's *Historia de la constitución de 1917* (2 vols. Mexico, D.F., 1938) are the two best general works on the 1917 Constitution.

57 Anónima, "La reorganización del ejército," in *El Universal,* May 9, 1925.

58 *El Universal,* May 9, 1925; Carranza, Message to Congress, Cámara de diputados, *Diario de debates,* April 15, 1917, p. 38.

59 *Diario de debates,* p. 39.

60 President Carranza, Message to Congress, Cámara de diputados, *Diario de debates,* Sept. 1, 1917, pp. 11-13; *El Universal,* May 9, 1925.

61 General Joaquín Aspiroz Viniergra, "La academia del estado mayor: primer escuela militar de la revolución," in *El Legionario,* November 1956, pp. 17-20.

62 General Juan Barragán, "El xxxi anniversario del ejército nacional," in *El Universal,* March 25, 1944.

63 President Carranza, Message to Congress, Cámara de diputados, *Diario de dabates,* Sept. 1, 1918, pp. 22-24.

64 Blasco Ibañez, pp. 192-99.

65 Article 73 of 1917 Constitution.

66 See Cámara de diputados, *Diario de debates* of Oct. 30, Nov. 10, and Dec. 26, 1917.

67 U.S. Military Attache, Campbell to War Dept., Mexico, D.F., April 24, 1918, ADS 812.00/10.

68 See Appendix A.

69 Marjorie Clark, *Organized Labor in Mexico* (Chapel Hill, Univ. of North Carolina Press, 1934), pp. 27-45.

70 *El Universal,* January 15, 1919.

71 *El Universal,* Mar. 30, 1919.

72 Consul Francis Dyer to Sec. of State, Nogales, May 21, 1919, ADS 812.00/22733.

73 *El Universal,* June 6, 1919.

74 Dulles, pp. 17-20.

75 Cited in Dulles, p. 22.

76 Summerlin to Sec. of State, Mexico, D.F., Jan. 21, 1920, ADS 812.00/23358.

77 Summerlin to Sec. of State, Mexico, D.F., May 21, 1919, ADS 812.00/22751; *El Monitor Republicano,* October 4, 1919.

78 Barragán, II: 469-477.

79 "El ejército nacional," in *El Legionario,* Aug. 1956, pp. 25-26.

80 "Carranza contra el militarismo," in *Todo,* Nov. 7, 1950.

81 González Ramírez, *La revolución social,* pp. 587-589.

82 Summerlin to Sec. of State, Mexico, D.F., Oct. 21, 1919, ADS 812.00/23182.

83 Blasco Ibañez, pp. 65-67, 121-123, 142-143.

84 Cristanti Cuellar Abaroa, "Carranza civilista," in *El Nacional,* May 22, 1954.

85 Luis N. Ruvulcaba (ed.), *Compaña política del Alvaro Obregón, 1919-1920. Compilación de documentos.* (Mexico, D.F., 1923), p. 54; Clark, pp. 72-73.

86 Dawson to Sec. of State, Tampico, Jan. 2, 1920, Summerlin to Sec. of State, Mexico, D.F., Feb. 2 and March 27, 1920, ADS 812.00/ 23324, 812.002/107, and 812.00/23430.

87 Dulles, pp. 24-25.

88 Plan of Agua Prieta, Agua Prieta, Sonora, April 23, 1920, in Naranjo, pp. 295-296.

89 Dulles, pp. 31-54; General Ignacio A. Richkarday, "El ejército debe ser siempre leal a las instituciones" in *Todo,* June 1, 1950.

90 González Ramírez, *La revolución social,* pp. 591-592; Frank Tannenbaum, *Mexico: the Struggle for Peace and Bread* (New York, Knopf, 1950), pp. 62-63.

91 For an analysis of this universal process see Edwards, pp. 118-120, 132-150, and Brinton, *The Anatomy of Revolution* (New York, Vintage, 1957), pp. 260-269.

NOTES TO CHAPTER THREE

1 Bojórquez, *Obregón,* pp. 12-13.

2 Bojórquez, p. 14; Ramón Puente, *Hombres de la revolución: O-bregón* (Los Angeles, 1933), pp. 181-183; Obregón, *Ocho mil kilometros en campaña,* p. 7-17.

3 Telegram, Obregón to Carranza, Puebla, January 12, 1915, reproduced in Barragán, II: 208.

4 Clark, pp. 97-105.

5 Dulles, pp. 93-101.

6 Robert Scott, *Mexican Government in Transition,* (Urbana, Univ. of Illinois Press, 1959), pp. 118-120.

7 *Excelsior,* July 16-22, 1920, Dulles, pp. 59-78.

8 General Juan Gualberto Amaya, *Los gobiernos de Obregón, Calles y regímenes "peleles" dirivados del Callismo* (Mexico, D.F., 1947), pp. 1-15.

9 Amaya, pp. 1-15; "Síntesis dictata por ... miembros del extinto Ejército Federal contra . . . el presidente," Mexico, D.F., March 1, 1922, in Archivo General de la Nación, Obregón, Papeles Presidenciales, Legajo 6-101-E-6. These are the papers of Floridablanca who was Secretary to Presidents Obregón and Calles. (Henceforth abreviated AGN/PP).

10 Official report on "Hacienda de concession de Canutillo," Mexico, D.F., Nov. 22, 1920, in Obregón, AGN/PP, Leg. 22-101-V-3.

11 For a fascinating exchange of telegrams between Obregón and Villa over these and other matters see Obregón AGN/PP, Leg. 22, 100-V-3 and V-11.

12 Amaya, pp. 27-32.

13 Summerlin to Sec. of State, Mexico, D.F., Dispatches of June 11 and July 15, 1921, Feb. 14 and 15, March 22, and June 7, 1922 in ADS 812.00/25053, 25109, 25358, 25401, and 25502.

14 Amaya, pp. 20-33; Dulles, pp. 113-118.

15 Cited in Tannenbaum, p. 63.

16 Gruening, p. 320.

17 Obregón, AGN/PP, memo of Sept. 22, 1921, and letter of Aug. 22, 1922 in Leg. 101-C-14 and 101-D-8.

8 Cámara de diputatos, *Diario de debates,* Dec. 12, 1921.

19 Brig. General Nicamón Pérez to Obregón, Veracruz, April 25, 1922, in AGN/PP, Leg. 101-A-11.

20 Pérez to Obregón, April 19, 1922, 101-A-31.

21 Director General de Correos to Obregón's Secretario Particular, AGN/PP, Leg. 8, 101-G-10, Oct. 2, 1922.

22 Letter of Nov. 16, 1922, AGN/PP, Leg. 8, 101-G-10.

23 Letter of April 7, 1923, AGN/PP, Leg. 19, 101-S-16.

24 Gen. Angel Flores to Obregón, Mazatlán, June 10, 1922, AGN/PP, Leg. 23, 101-Y-2; Secretary Particular to Sec. de Guerra, AGN/PP, Leg. 8, 104-G.—44; Brig. Gen. Luis T. Mirelu to Obregón, Villahermosa, Sept. 3, 1922, AGN/PP, Leg. 14, 101-M-2.

25 Summerlin to Sec. of State, Mexico, D.F., ADS 812.00/25845.

26 Examples of such complaints can be found in Obregon, AGN/PP, Leg. 8, 101-G-2 (Sept. 17, 1921), 101-B-6 (Oct. 31, 1922), Legajo 4,100-M-35 (Aug. 5, 1922), and Leg. 18, 101-R-2 (Mar. 31, 1922).

27 AGN/PP, May 29, 1923, Leg. 18, 101-R-6; Aug. 9, 1923, Leg. 8, 101-G-18; Aug. 21, 1923, Leg. 15, 101-N-4.

28 *Excelsior,* Feb. 10, 1922.

29 Summerlin to Sec. of State, Mexico, D.F., Dec. 29, 1922 ADS 812.00/26162. In Nayarit, the military governor, General Pascual Villanueva, fought with the Jefe de Operaciones.

30 *El Universal* (editorial), June 19, 1920; Obregón, "Proyecto de reformas de la ordenanza del ejército," in AGN/PP, Leg. 1, 731-E-6.

31 Cámara de Diputados, *Diario de debates,* Dec. 17, 1920.

32 "La primera reserva del ejército," (editorial), *El Heraldo de Mexico,* Sept. 27, 1921.

33 General Saturnino Cedillo to Obregón, San Luis Pososí, Feb. 20, 1922, General Eulalio Gutiérrez to Obregón, Mexico, D.F., Nov. 3, 1922, and General Arcadio P. Figueroa to Obregón (telegram), Sept. 17, 1923, in AGN/PP, Leg. 3, 101-C-10, 14, 101-M-22, and 7, 100-F-9.

34 Cámara de diputados, *Diario de debates,* Dec. 17, 1920. Provision in the law was also made for loans of up to fifteen thousand pesos to purchase agricultural implements.

35 Message to Congress in *Diario de debates,* Sept. 1, 1921; Roberto Quiros Martínez, *Alvaro Obregón* (Mexico, D.F., 1928), pp. 195-200; Summerlin to Sec. of State, Mexico, D.F., Feb. 24, 1923, ADS 812.00/43.

36 See Appendix A.

37 Portes Gil, pp. 237-238.

38 War Minister General Enrique Estrada to Obregón, AGN/

PP, Leg. 7, 101-F-12. Officers pay ranged from twenty pesos daily for a brigadier general to five pesos daily for a captain.

39 In early 1923, the cavalry numbered 31,000, the infantry 29,000. Summerlin to Sec. of State, Mexico, D.F., Feb. 24, 1923, ADS 812.20/43.

40 See Secretario de Guerra, *Memoria y Cuenta,* 1907 and 1921.

41 *Diario Oficial,* Feb. 23, 1923.

42 Another important factor conflicting with the aim of rendering the army apolitical was the insistence of the Agua Prieta victors upon defending their rebellion as a social mission, that is, to defend the principles of the Revolution in behalf of the Mexican people. In other words, the Obregonistas encouraged an identity between the functions of the army and the aspirations of the proletariat. The idealistic viewpoint espoused was that Agua Prieta represented the armed populace fighting for their social rights against the forces of reaction. See Enrique L. Calderón, "La revolución y el ejército," in *El Nacional,* November 14, 1957.

A more cynical view of Obregón's efforts to build an apolitical army came from General Salvador Alvarado, one of the vanquished in the Agua Prieta rebellion. He saw Obregón's army as nothing more than a political tool used to maintain and to increase the personal power of President Alvaro Obregón, to see that the official candidates always won the elections, and to keep the opposition down by force. To Alvarado there was little difference in the use Díaz and Obregón made of their armies. See Alvarado's *The Fundamental Problem of Mexico* (San Antonio, Texas, 1920), pp. 15-19.

43 Generals Turbicio Ruiz in Chiapas, Luis Guitiérrez in Coahuila, Enrique Natera in Durango, Francisco Figueroa in Guerrero, Nicholas Flores in Hidalgo, Francisco Mújica in Michoacán, Abundio Gómez in Mexico, Angel Flores in Sinaloa, and Octavio Solís in Quintana Roo.

44 Summerlin to Sec. of State, Mexico, D.F., Dec. 29, 1922, ADS 812.00/26162.

45 Col. Villa of the Piedras Negras Garrison violated this order by talking to refugee politicians in Texas and was relieved of his command. Obregón to General Joaquín Amaro, Mexico, D.F., July 25, 1921, AGN/PP, Leg. 22, 101-V-4.

46 Summerlin to Sec. of State, Mexico, D.F., April 11, 1922, ADS 812.00/25538.

47 *Excelsior,* July 11, 1923; General de Brigada Francisco Saavedra to Obregón, Cuernavaca, Sept. 22, 1923, AGN/PP, Leg. 6, 101-R-2-E.

48 Quiros Martínez, op. cit., pp. 94-95; Gabried Cuevas, *El glorioso colegio militar en su siglo (1824-1924)* (Mexico, D.F., 1942), pp. 167-198.

49 "Departamento del estado mayor del ejército," in *El Heraldo de Mexico,* Sept. 27, 1921; Cámara de diputados, *Diario de debates,* Dec. 5, 1921. In these technical matters the services of General Maciel, a former Federal Army officer, were put to good use.

50 Fritz Epstein, "Foreign Military Missions in Latin America" (Manuscript in Library of Congress, Washington, 1944), p. 206.

51 Cámara de diputados, *Diario de debates,* March 17, 1921; Obregón to Sec. de Guerra, Mexico, D.F., July 8, 1921, AGN/UG Pp, Leg. 6, 101-E-13. Obregón as president always wore civilian clothing, and in his crumpled grey suit his bearing was most unmilitary.

52 Cámara de diputados, *Diario de debates,* Dec. 17, 1920, and Sept. 1, 1921.

53 González Ramirez, *Planes politicos,* p. xiviii.

54 Quiros Martínez, p. 200.

55 Portes Gil, p. 240.

56 For the universal nature of the warrior psychology of amateur generals in the aftermath of a social revolution, see Georges Sorel, *Reflections on Violence* (New York, Crowell-Collier, 1961), pp. 166-167.

57 Congress of Guerrero to Obregón, Chilpancingo, Nov. 19, 1923, and L. Villegas to Obregón, Mexico, D.F., April 16, 1923, AGN/PP, Leg. 8, 101-6-21 and 101-E-12.

58 Clark, pp. 100-102.

59 Dulles, pp. 128-135; Scott, p. 119.

60 *El Heraldo,* March 16, 1923; *Excelsior,* March 23, 1923; Summerlin to Sec. of State, Mexico, D.F., 812.20/56.

61 Portes Gil, pp. 240-241; Dulles, pp. 173-174, 208.

62 *El Heraldo,* June 14, 1923.

63 Summerlin to Sec. of State, Mexico, D.F., Sept. 28, 1923, ADS 821.00/26467.

64 Summerlin to Sec. of State, Aug. 29, 1923, ADS 812.00/26449.

65 Dulles, pp. 182-217. Dulles states that more than half the army rebelled, but official figures do not bear this out.

66 Amaya, pp. 35-36.

67 Telegram reproduced in Amaya, pp. 36-40.

68 Message to Congress, Cámara de diputados, *Diario de debates,* Sept. 1, 1924, pp. 25-26.

69 *Diario de debates,* Sept. 1, 1924, pp. 26-27.

70 The standard works on the 1923 rebellion are Alonso Capetillo, *La rebelión sin cabeza* (Mexico, D.F., 1925) and Luis Monroy Durán *El último caudillo* (Mexico, D.F., 1924). The best account in English can be found in Dulles, pp. 218-263. Adolfo de la Huerta, *Memorias* (Mexico, D.F., 1957) is the most important primary source on the rebellion.

71 Capetillo, pp. 112, 134-137.

72 Message to Congress, Cámara de diputados, *Diario de debates,* Sept. 1, 1924, pp. 27-28.

73 Rebel practices were more humane in this respect. For example, the lives of two future presidents (Cárdenas and Avila Camacho) were spared by rebel leaders following the capture of these two on the field of battle. See Dulles, p. 241.

74 Gruening, pp. 321-322.

75 Antonio Islas Bravo, *La succesión presidential de 1928* (Mexico, D.F., 1927), pp. 28-29.

76 These and other representative claims may be examined in Obregón, AGN/PP, May 17, 1924, Leg. 3, 101-C-8, July 4, 1924, Leg. 7, 101-F-5, and Aug. 29, 1924, Leg. 6, 101-R2-4.

77 Obregón to General Eugenio Martínez, Mexico, D.F., July 4, 1924, AGN/PP, Leg. 14, 191-M-44.

78 Telegram to Obregón, Tepic, Aug. 16, 1924, Leg. 16, 101-0-4.

79 Articles 106-117, Cámara de diputados, *Diario de debates,* Sept. 11, 1924.

80 Secretary of War (Serrano) to Obregón, Mexico, D.F., April 29, 1924, AGN/PP, Leg. 8, 101-G-23.

NOTES TO CHAPTER FOUR

1 Luciano Kubli, *Calles: el hombre y su gobierno* (Mexico, D.F., 1931), pp. 62-86; Juan de Dios Bojórquez, *Calles* (Mexico, D.F., 1925), pp. 53-65; Puente, *Hombres de la revolución,* pp. 370-373.

2 Clark, pp. 102-120.

3 Dulles, pp. 264-283.

4 Consul Paul Foster to Sec. of State, Salina Cruz, Sept. 7, 1926, ADS 812.22/6.

5 Gonzáles Ramírez, *Planes Políticos,* pp. 280-294.

6 For photographs that reveal the brutalities, see Anita Brenner, *The Wind that Swept Mexico* (New York, Harper, 1943), Illustrations 133-134.

7 While a number of revolutionary generals, particularly Juan Andreu Almazán, thought Calles wrong in persecuting the Church, they all opposed the Cristero movement, for it included all the counter-revolutionary forces—landholders, federales, and foreign interests, such as the Knights of Columbus, as well as the Church.

8 Lt. Col. Davis, Mil. Attache to War Dept., Mexico, D.F., Dec. 31, 1926, ADS 812.00/2153.

9 General Onofre Jiménez, Governor of Oaxaca to Calles, Oaxaca, May 18, 1925, AGN/PP, Leg. 6, 101-0-12.

10 Gruening, pp. 322-331.

11 Carleton Beals, "The Indian who Sways Mexican Destiny," *New York Times Magazine,* Dec. 7, 1930, pp. 8, ff.

12 For obvious reasons, no newspaper in Mexico City dared report the incident. Scheffield to State, Mexico, D.F., Oct. 21, 1925, ADS 812.002/191.

13 Illustrative is the case of General Alfredo Serratos, a Mexican consul in Detroit and St. Louis under Obregón. For several years Amaro frustrated his repeated efforts to get back on active duty. See AGN/PP, Leg. 7, 101-S-18 and Leg. 19, 101-S-18.

14 Secretaría de Guerra y Marina, *Memoria,* 1930/31, p. 10.

15 See Appendix A.

16 Secretaría de Guerra y Marina, *Memoria,* 1930/31; p. 10.

17 *Diario Oficial,* March 15, 1926.

18 *Diario Oficial,* March 15, 1926; *La Patria,* Oct. 16, 1926.

19 *Diario Oficial,* Mar. 15, 1926; Guening, p. 320; *La Patria,* Oct. 23, 1926.

20 *Diario Oficial,* Mar. 15, 1926; *La Patria,* Nov. 6, 1926.

21 Sec. de Guerra to Obregón, Mexico, D.F., April 29, 1924, AGN/PP, Leg. 8-101-G-23.

22 Cited in Gruening, p. 232; Sec. de Guerra, Circulars of April 24, 1926 and April 7, 1927.

23 Detailed information on these complaints can be found in

AGN/PP, Leg. 18, 101-R-25 (Feb. 18, 1925), Leg. 1, 10-R-12A (January 26, 1926), Leg. 21, 101-U-1 (August 3, 1928), and Leg. 7, 101-C-28 (Sept. 19, 1928).

24 *Diario de Yucatán,* Aug. 19-20, 1948.

25 *Diario de Yucatán,* Aug. 1, 1948. Amaro's fear of having his properties confiscated probably kept him from rebellion in the late 1930's when he was stripped of his political power.

26 *Diario de Yucatán,* Aug. 1, 19, 29-30, 1948.

27 *Diario de Yucatán,* Sept. 8 and July 31, 1948; Clark to Sec. of State, Mexico, D.F., Nov. 13, 1931, ADS, 812.20/94.

28 *Diario de Yucatán,* Aug. 25, Sept. 3, 4, and 10, 1948.

29 Lucio Mendieta y Muñez, "Los civiles de la revolución," *El Universal,* May 9, 1945; *Diario de Yucatán,* Aug. 29, 1948.

30 Ricardo Calderón Arizmendi, *Síntesis de la revolución mexicana* (Santiago, 1929), pp. 218-220.

31 Capitan José Galván Cantú, "La obra de Señores Generales Calles y Amaro en pro de la reorganización y perfeccionamiento del ejército," *Revista de Ejército,* April, 1930, pp. 269-272.

32 Consul General Wedell to Sec. of State, Mexico, D.F., July 21, 1925, ADS 812.20/64.

33 Ten. Col. Francisco Lazcano, "Porque fracasó el Colegio Militar," *Excelsior,* Oct. 14, 1924; Anónimo, "La enseñanza militar y la revolución," *Escelsior,* Oct. 19, 1925.

34 Cantú, pp. 271-272; Sec. de Guerra, *Memoria,* 1930.31, pp. 9-10; Sec. de Guerra, *Los estudios de la escuela superior de guerra* (Mexico, D.F., 1934) , pp. 24-25, 65, 73-175.

35 Anónimo, "Personalidad de General Joaquín Amaro," *El Legionario,* March 1952, pp. 4-10.

36 *New York Times Magazine,* Dec. 7, 1930, p. 8; Virginia Prewitt, *Reportage on Mexico* (New York, Dutton, 1941), p. 76.

37 Cantú, pp. 269-272.

38 G. A. Salas (ed.) "La successión presidencial y el ejército," *Excelsior,* June 15, 1927; Col. F. J. Aguilar, "La reorganización de Ejército Nacional," *El Demócrata,* August 9, 1925.

39 Calderón Arizmendi, pp. 222-224; Cantú, p. 272; Calles, Presidential messages of 1926 and 1927, Cámara de diputados, *Diario de debates,* Sept. 1, 1926, p. 13 and Sept. 1, 1927, p. 10.

40 *New York Times Magazine,* Dec. 7, 1930, p. 8.

41 Summerlin to Sec. of State, Mexico, D.F., July 30, 1925, ADS 812.00/27579.

42 Sheffield to Sec. of State, Mexico, D.F., Mar. 12, 1926, ADS 812.00/27736.

43 Puente, pp. 220-222.

44 Sheffield to Sec. of State, Mexico, D.F., May 29, 1926, ADS 812.002/192.

45 Dulles, pp. 333-334.

46 Sheffield to Sec. of State, Mexico, D.F., Feb. 2, 1927, ADS 812.00/28224.

47 Sheffeld to Sec. of State, Mexico, D.F., April 7, 1927, ADS 812.00/28312.

48 *Revista del Ejército*, May 1927, pp. 340-342.

49 See *Excelsior* editorial of June 23, 1927.

50 Clark, pp. 121-128.

51 Dulles, pp. 335-336.

52 Amaya, p. 142.

53 Puente, p. 223.

54 Miguel Alessio Robles, *Historia política de la revolución*, (Mexico, D.F., 1946), pp. 385-391. When Serrano was captured General Roberto Cruz had qualms about following out Obregón's order to shoot such a close friend, so General Claudio Fox was called in to do the job.

55 Sheffield to Sec. of State, Mexico, D.F., Oct. 18, 1927, ADS 812.00/28906; Johnson to Sec. of State, Torreón, Oct. 10, 1927, ADS 812.00/28825.

56 *Excelsior*, Oct. 11, 1927. The *divisionarios* involved, in addition to Serrano and Gómez, were Jacinto B. Treviño and Luis Gutiérrez. Eugenio Martínez was also implicated, but escaped death by being transferred to a post abroad before the uprising took place.

57 *Excelsior*, July 30, 1928.

58 Cámara de diputados, *Diario de debates,* Sept. 1, 1928, pp. 5 ff.

59 Morrow to Sec. of State, Mexico, D.F., Sept. 3, 1928, ADS 812.00/29309.

60 The sensational revelations of how the generals held private court on the succession problems were revealed in Froylán C. Manjarrez, *La jornada institucional* (2 vols., Mexico, D.F., 1930), I: 41-69.

61 Manjarrez, I: 43-69; Antonio Enríquez Filio, "El ejército y la

succession presidencial," *Excelsior* (editorial), March 14, 1930; *El Universal*, January 27, 1930.

62 Manjarrez, I; 58-69.

63 In Edward Gibbon's famous description of political activities of the praetorian guard in Augustinian Rome he describes how "the emperor was elected by the authority of the senate, and the consent of the soldiers." The situation in Mexico had striking parallels.

64 Dulles, p. 405.

65 *Excelsior*, Dec. 5, 1928.

66 Scott, pp. 121-123; Dulles, pp. 427-434.

67 Frank Brandenburg, "Mexico: an Experiment in One-Party Democracy," (Ph.D. thesis, unpublished, Philadelphia, Univ. of Pennsylvania, 1956), pp. 57-58.

68 Articles 1, 13, 14 of Plan of Hermosillo in Naranjo, pp. 298-299.

69 Portes Gil, p. 279.

70 Alfonso León de Garay, *El palpitar de la casta* (Puebla, 1929), pp. 9-11.

71 *New York Times*, April 6, 1930, p. 11.

72 Presidential message to Congress, Cámara de deputados, *Diario de debates*, Sept. 1, 1932, p. 25.

73 Daniels to Sec. of State, Mexico, D.F., Oct. 31, 1933, ADS 812.20/119; *New York Times*, Nov. 1, 1933, p. 11.

74 Ricardo Calderón Serrano, *El ejército y sus tribunales* (Mexico, D.F., 1944), pp. 113-114; Cámara de diputados, *Diario de debates*, Dec. 14, 1933, pp. 3-4. Under the law, an officer was allowed to resign temporarily in order to engage in a political campaign, provided he reentered the service as soon as the election was over, if he lost, or as soon as his term of political office ended, if he won.

75 Lane to Sec. of State, Mexico, D.F., Oct. 16, 1930, ADS 812.00/29527.

76 Clark, pp. 134-140; Scott, pp. 122-123.

77 Scott, pp. 122-123.

78 *Excelsior*, Dec. 10, 1928.

79 Dulles, pp. 478-479.

80 Lane to Sec. of State, Mexico, D.F., Oct. 16, 1930, ADS 812.00/29527; *New York Times Magazine*, Dec. 7, 1930, p. 8.

81 Scott, pp. 122-123.

82 Scott, pp. 124-125.

83 Hawks to Sec. of State, Mexico, D.F., Mar. 24, 1933, ADS 813.00/29834.

84 Military Attache Gordon Johnston, G-2 report, Mexico, D.F., Feb. 10, 1931, ADS 812.00/29595.

85 Dulles, pp. 488-542.

86 Dulles, pp. 544-557.

87 Scott, p. 125.

88 Dulles, pp. 572-604.

89 See Appendix A.

90 *Diario Oficial,* Aug. 5 and 29, 1931.

91 *El Nacional,* Jan. 16, 1933; *El Universal,* Jan. 21, 1933. Cárdenas reduced the cavalry regiments from 72 to 42 in 1933.

92 Presidential message, Cámara de disputados, *Diario de debates,* Sept. 1, 1932, pp. 24-25; Sec. de Guerra, *Memoria,* 1930/1931, p. 10.

93 Secretario de Guerra, *Memoria,* 1930-1933; Luis Franco, *Tres años de historia del ejército de Mexico,* 1930-1932 (Mexico, D.F., 1946), pp. 35-38.

94 Roberto Quiros Martínez, *Abelardo L. Rodríguez* (Mexico, D.F., 1934).

95 Dirección General de Educación Militar, *Los estudios de la Escuela Superior* (Mexico, D.F., 1934), pp. 25-65; Luis Alamillo Flores, *Doctrina mexicana de guerra* (Mexico, D.F., 1943), pp. 23-96.

96 Sec. de Guerra, *Memoria,* 1930/1931, p. 10, 1932/1933, p. 14; Prewitt, p. 614.

97 *Revista del ejército,* June, 1931, pp. 420-421; *El Nacional,* Oct. 8, 1931.

98 Francisco Javier Gaxiola, *El Presidente Rodríguez* (Mexico, D.F., 1938), pp. 277-282.

NOTES TO CHAPTER FIVE

1 See editorial in *Excelsior,* Oct. 27, 1930.

2 *El Nacional,* May 17, 1933.

3 Daniels to Sec. of State, Mexico, D.F., Aug. 17, 1933, ADS 812.00/29909.

4 Juan de Dios Bojórquez, *Lázaro Cárdenas,* (Mexico, D.F., 1933), pp. 119-120; William C. Townsend, *Lázaro Cárdenas* (Ann Arbor, Univ. of Michigan Press, 1952), p. 72.

5 *New York Times,* July 5, 1934, p. 4.

6 Dulles, pp. 606-607, 625-626.

7 R. Henry Noweb, Charge d'affaires to Sec. of State, Mexico, D.F., Jan. 17, 1936, ADS 812.00/30329.

8 Noweb to Sec. of State, Mexico, D.F., Jan. 17, 1936, ADS 812.00/ 30329.

9 Daniels to Sec. of State, Mexico, D.F., June 18, 1935, ADS 812.00/30225; *New York Times,* June 23, 1935, IV: 11.

10 *New York Times,* June 23, 1935, IV: 11.

11 Walter Mallory (ed.), *Political Handbook of the World* (New York, Council on Foreign Relations, 1935), pp. 126-127.

12 Gabriel García Maroto, *Hombre del pueblo* (Mexico, D.F., 1940), p. 70; *New York Times,* Dec. 11, 1935, p. 21.

13 *New York Times,* April 11, 1936, p. 1; Dulles, pp. 662-680.

14 Sec. de Guerra y Marina, *Memoria,* 1933/34, p. 10.

15 Sec. de Guerra y Marina, *Memoria,* 1934/35, p. 14, and 1935/ 36, p. 16; Mexico, Presidente, *Reglamento general de deberes militares* (Mexico, D.F., 1936) ; Virginia Prewitt, "The Mexican Army," in *Foreign Affairs,* April, 1941, p. 614.

16 Message to Congress, Cámara de diputados, *Diario de debates,* Sept. 1, 1935, pp. 8-9; García Maroto, pp. 269-273.

17 *Diario de debates,* Sept. 1, 1935, pp. 8-9.

18 See Appendix A.

19 José Mijares Palencia, *El gobierno mejicano* (Mexico, D.F., 1936), pp. 93-99; García Maroto, pp. 271-272.

20 Message to Congress, Cámara de diputados, *Diario de debates,* Sept. 1, 1935, pp. 8-9.

21 This was achieved by an April 27, 1935 decree establishing a Dirección de Materias de Guerra, which branch also trained soldiers to work in the military factories. See García Maroto, pp. 209-270.

22 *Revista del ejército,* Jan. 1936, pp. 3-5.

23 García Maroto, pp. 270-271.

24 Quoted in José Mansilla Cortes, *Justicia al soldado* (Mexico, 1952), p. 46.

25 García Maroto, pp. 272-273; Major Olegario González Macías, "El servicio militar nacional," in *El Legionario,* Aug., 1954, p. 49; General Rubén García, "El Ejército Nacional," in *El Legionario,* Aug., 1956, pp. 25-26.

26 *New York Times,* July 18, 1935, p. 7, Aug. 17, 1935, p. 2.

27 Daniels to Sec. of State, Mexico, D.F., Dec. 10, 1936, ADS 812.00/30329.

28 *El Nacional,* Sept. 22, 1936.

29 *El Universal,* July 14, 1937.

30 Daniels to Sec. of State, Mexico, D.F., July 21, 1937, ADS 812.00/30470.

31 Mexico, Partido de la Revolución Mexicana (PRM) *Pacto constitutivo, declaración de principios, programa y estatutos* (Mexico, D.F., 1938).

32 PRM, *Informe del Secretaría de Defensa Nacional* (Mexico, D.F., 1938), pp. 3.

33 PRM, *Informa del Secretaría de Defensa Nacional,* p. 4.

34 Daniels to Sec. of State, Mexico, D.F., Feb. 11, 1938, ADS 812.00/30532.

35 PRM, *Informe del Secretaría de Defensa Nacional,* (1938), p. 13.

36 Prewitt, p. 167; Brandenburg, pp. 88-90.

37 Quoted in Townsend, p 216.

38 PRM, *Informe del Secretaria de Denfensa Nacional* (1938), pp. 3-7.

39 Brandenburg, pp. 89.

40 Brandenburg, pp. 98-99.

41 *New York Times,* Aug. 17, 1937, p. 1.

42 *New York Times,* May 2, 1938, p. 1.

43 *New York Times,* June 30, 1938.

44 Daniels to Sec. of State, Mexico, D.F., Aug. 5, 1938, ADS 812.00/30609; *New York Times,* July 17, 1938, p. 22.

45 *New York Times,* August 11, 1938, p. 6.

46 Consul General William Blocher to Sec. of State, Ciudad Juárez, Aug. 12, 1938, ADS 812.00/30608; *New York Times,* Oct. 16, 1938, p. 33.

47 Frente Constitucional Democrático, "Manifesto," October 1938 broadside; *Excelsior,* Dec. 8, 1938.

48 See Ramón Verduzco, "Propaganda reaccionaria en el ejército," in *Diario del Sureste* (Mérida, Yucatán), Sept. 21, 1938.

49 Daniels to Sec. of State, Mexico, D.F., Feb. 14, 1939, ADS 812.00/30696.

50 Daniels to Sec. of State, Mexico, D.F., Feb. 14, 1939, ADS 812.00/30696.

51 *New York Times,* Feb. 19, 1939, p. 27.

52 *New York Times,* Feb. 19, 1939, p. 27.

53 For this analysis of the pressures operative inside the PRM I am indebted to the research of Marta Hunt. See her "The Mexican Presidential Election of 1940," (M.A. thesis, unpublished, Albuquerque, Univ. of New Mexico, 1962), pp. 58-106.

54 Hunt, pp. 58-106.

55 Prewitt, pp. 175-176.

56 Prewitt, pp. 188-190; *El Nacional,* Mar. 10, 1939, *Excelsior,* Mar. 11, 1939.

57 *Excelsior,* Jan. 31, 1939.

58 Ramón Verduzco, "El ejército y sus demandas" in *Diario del Sureste,* Mar. 24, 1939.

59 *El Universal,* Mar. 13, 1939.

60 Hunt, pp. 58-75. Magaña died of illness in December of 1939.

61 Hunt, pp. 62-99; Memorandum, Lawrence Duggan to Sumner Welles, Washington, June 19, 1939, ADS 812.00/30767.

62 José C. Valades, "Millionarios de la Revolución: Juan Andreu Almazán," in *Diario de Yucatán,* July 31, 1948; G-2 Report, Lt. Col. Gordon McCoy to War Dept., Mexico, D.F., Aug. 1, 1939, ADS 812.00/30819.

63 Hunt, pp. 106-120.

64 Hunt, pp. 90-101; see my *Arms and Politics in Latin America,* (New York, Praeger, 1960), pp. 116-117. Leaders of the Almazán campaign committee were Generals Emilio Madero, Marcelo Caraveo, Jacinto B. Treviño, Roberto Cruz, Ramón Iturbe, Espiridion Rodríguez, Francisco Coss, and Mijares Palencia. Daniels to Sec. of State, Mexico, D.F., Aug. 27, 1940, ADS 812.00/31349.

65 Daniels to Sec. of State, Mexico, D.F., June 20, 1939, ADS 812.00/30752.

66 *Excelsior,* Sept. 5, 1939.

67 General Francisco Urquizo, "Hace quince años," in *Mañana,* Jan. 22, 1955, p. 223; Daniels to Sec. of State, Mexico, D.F., Feb. 2, 1940, ADS 812.00/30927.

68 *New York Times,* Jan. 4, 1940, p. 11 and Feb. 12, 1940, p. 3.

69 Betty Kirk, "Mexico Moves Right," in *Washington Post,* May 14, 1940.

70 *Excelsior,* June 11, 1940.

71 *New York Times,* July 4, 1940, p. 4; *La Prensa,* June 25, 1940; *Excelsior,* July 3, 1940.

72 General Francisco Urquizo, "Hace quince años," in *Mañana,* Jan. 22, 1955, p. 223.

73 *Excelsior,* July 8, 1940; Daniels to Sec. of State, Mexico, D.F., July 7, 1940, ADS 812.00/31138.

74 *Excelsior,* July 13, 1940.

75 *Excelsior,* July 18, 1940.

76 General Juan Andreu Almazán, *Memorias* (Mexico, D.F., 1958), p. 125.

77 Daniels to Sec. of State, Mexico, D.F., Aug. 2, 1940, ADS 812.00/31272.

78 *New York Times,* Aug. 11, 1940, p. 16 and Aug. 20, 1940, p. 3.

79 *Excelsior,* Aug. 10 and 29, 1940.

80 Cámara de diputados, *Diario de debates,* Sept. 1, 1940, pp. 20-21.

81 Associated Press, New York, Sept. 2, 1940; reprinted in *Excelsior,* Sept. 4, 1940.

82 *El Nacional,* Sept. 13, 1940.

83 *Excelsior,* Sept. 11 & Oct. 2, 1940; *New York Times,* Sept. 14, 1940, p. 5, Oct. 2, 1940, p. 1, Oct. 3, 1940, p. 3. Almazanista General Andrés Zargosa was killed in the Monterrey skirmish.

84 *El Nacional,* Oct. 4, 1940; Daniels to Sec. of State, Mexico, D.F., Oct. 17, 1940, ADS 812.00/240; Prewitt, pp. 240-241. Mexico's air force, where Almazanista sympathies had been strong, was placated with twenty-seven new planes. See *New York Times,* Sept. 2, 1940.

85 *El Universal,* Oct. 20, 1940; *Excelsior,* Nov. 17, 1940.

86 *Excelsior,* Nov. 27-29, 1940.

NOTES TO CHAPTER SIX

1 The table and budget figures have been compiled from Secretaría de Hacienda, *Presupuesto Anual,* 1940-1966.

2 See James W. Wilkie, *The Mexican Revolution: Federal Expenditure and Social Change Since 1910* (Berkeley, Univ. of Calif. Press, 1967), pp. 22-23, 100-106, 293.

3 Brandenburg, 236-237.

4 Howard Cline, *The United States and Mexico* (Cambridge, Mass., Harvard Univ. Press, 1953) , p. 276.

5 Cline, pp. 277-278.

6 *Excelsior,* July 4, 1945; *New York Times,* July 5, 1945, p. 5.

7 Juan Barragán, "Los cuadros del ejército," *El Universal,* 28 July 1945.

8 John C. Drier, *The Organization of American States and the Hemisphere Crisis* (New York, Harper and Row, 1962), pp. 43-48.

9 Lieuwen, pp. 200-201; *Hispanic American Report,* Jan. 1952, p. 8, July 1953, p. 10.

10 *New York Times,* April 15, 1952, p. 5, April 18, 1952, p. 5.

11 Tucker, p. 196.

12 Several reputable scholars of the contemporary Mexican scene have been reluctant to write off the political influence of the Mexican military. Howard F. Cline in his *Mexico; Revolution to Evolution, 1940-1960* (New York, Oxford, 1962), p. 175, states that the military is still "one of several interest groups" in the political power complex. Frank R. Brandenburg, in his *The Making of Modern Mexico* (Englewood Cliffs, N.J., Prentice Hall, 1964), pp. 93-94, declares that unmistakable evidence of the army's political power is "the fact that an army general has held the party presidency uninterruptedly since 1946, while dozens of military men have become governors." Scott, p. 134, believes that "the military continues to wield a very important influence in policy making."

BIBLIOGRAPHY

ARCHIVES

United States, Department of State, *Diplomatic correspondence and papers relating to Mexico,* 1911-1940.

Mexico, Archivo General de la Nación, *Papeles Presidentiales de Obregón y Calles* (Floridablanca papers), 1920-1928.

DOCUMENTS

Mexico, Cámara de diputados, *Diario de debates,* 1917-1940.

Mexico, *Diario Oficial,* 1923-1931.

Mexico, Presidente, *Reglamento general de deberes militares* (Mexico, D.F., 1936).

Mexico, Secretaría de Guerra, *Los estudios de la escuela superior de guerra* (Mexico, D.F., 1934).

Mexico, Secretaría de Guerra, *Memoria y Cuenta,* 1907-1934.

Mexico, Secretaría de Guerra, Dirección General de Educación Militar, *Los estudios de la Escuela Superior* (Mexico, D.F., 1934).

Mexico, Secretaría de Hacienda, *Presupuesto Anual,* 1910-1964.

Partido de la Revolución Mexicana, *Informe de Secretario de Defensa Nacional* (Mexico, D.F., 1935).

Partido de la Revolución Mexicana, *Pacto constitutivo, declaración de principios, programa y estatutos* (Mexico, D.F., 1938).

BIBLIOGRAPHY

BOOKS

Alamillo Flores, Luis. *Doctrina mexicana de guerra* (Mexico, D.F., 1943).

Alessio Robles, Miguel. *Historia política de la revolución* (Mexico, D.F., 1946).

Almazan, Juan Andreu. *Memorias* (Mexico, D.F., 1958).

Alvarado, Salvador. *The Fundamental Problems of Mexico* (San Antonio, 1920).

Amaya, Juan Gualberto. *Los gobiernos de Obregón, Calles, y régimes "peleles" dirivados del Callismo* (Mexico, D.F., 1947).

Barragán Rodríguez, Juan. *Historia del ejército y de la Revolución Constitutionalista* (2 vols, Mexico, D.F., 1946).

Beals, Carleton. *Porfirio Díaz* (Philadelphia, Lippencott, 1932).

Blasco Ibañez, Vicente. *El militarismo mejicano* (Valencia, Prometeo, 1920).

Bojórquez, Juan de Dios. *Calles* (Mexico, D.F., 1925).

Bojórquez, Juan de Dios. *Crónica del constituyente* (Mexico, D.F., 1938).

Bojórquez, Juan de Dios. *Lázaro Cárdenas* (Mexico, D.M., 1933).

Bojórquez, Juan de Dios. *Obregón, apuntes biográficas* (Mexico, D.F., 1929).

Brandenburg, Frank. *The Making of Modern Mexico* (Englewood Cliffs, Prentice Hall, 1964).

Brandenburg, Frank. *Mexico: an Experiment in One-Party Democracy* (Philadelphia, University of Pennsylvania Ph.D. Thesis, unpublished, 1956).

Brenner, Anita. *The Wind that Swept Mexico* (New York, Harper, 1943).

Brinton, Crane. *The Anatomy of Revolution* (New York, Vintage, 1957).

Calderón, Arizmendi, Ricardo. *Síntesis de la revolución mexicana* (Santiago, 1929).

Calderón Serrano, Ricardo. *El ejército y sus tribunales* (Mexico, D.F., 1944).

Capetillo, Alonso. *La rebelión sin cabeza* (Mexico, D.F., 1925).

Clark, Marjorie. *Organized Labor in Mexico* (Chapel Hill, University of North Carolina Press, 1934).

BIBLIOGRAPHY

Clenendon, Clarence C. *The United States and Pancho Villa* (Ithaca, Cornell University Press, 1961).

Cline, Howard F. *Mexico: Revolution to Evolution 1940-1960* (New York, Oxford, 1962).

Cline, Howard F. *The United States and Mexico* (Cambridge, Harvard University Press, 1953).

Cuevas, Gabriel. *El glorioso colegio militar en su siglo (1824-1924)* (Mexico, D.F., 1924).

Cumberland, Charles. *The Mexican Revolution: Genesis under Madero* (Austin, University of Texas Press, 1952).

de la Huerta, Adolfo. *Memorias* (Mexico, D.F., 1957).

Drier, John C. *The Organization of American States and the Hemisphere Crisis* (New York, Harper and Row, 1962).

Dulles, John W. F. *Yesterday in Mexico* (Austin, University of Texas Press, 1961).

Edwards, Lyford P. *The Natural History of Revolution* (Chicago, University of Chicago Press, 1927).

Epstein, Fritz. *Foreign Military Missions in Latin America* (Washington, Library of Congress Manuscript, 1944).

Fornaro, Walter. *Carranza and Mexico* (New York, Kennedy, 1915).

Franco, Luis. *Tres años de historia del ejército de Mexico, 1930-1932* (Mexico, D.F., 1946).

García Maroto, Gabriel. *Hombre del pueblo* (Mexico, D.F., 1940).

Gaxiola, Francisco Javier. *El Presidente Rodríguez* (Mexico, D.F., 1938).

González Ramírez, Manuel. *Planes políticos y otros documentos* Mexico, D.F., 1954).

González Ramírez, Manuel. *La revolución en México* (Mexico, D.F., 1960).

Greenleaf, Richard and Sherman, William. *Victoriano Huerta: a Reappraisal* (Mexico, D.F., 1960).

Gruening, Ernest. *Mexico and its Heritage* (New York, Appleton-Century, 1928).

Hunt, Marta. *The Mexican Presidential Election of 1940.* (Albuquerque, University of New Mexico M.A. thesis, unpublished, 1962).

Islas Bravo, Antonio. *La sucessión presidencial en 1928* (Mexico, D.F., 1927).

Janvier, Thomas A. *The Armies of Today* (New York, 1893).

Jerram, Charles M. *Armies of the World* (London, 1899).

BIBLIOGRAPHY

Kubli, Luciano, *Calles: el hombre y su gobierno* (Mexico, D.F., 1931).

León de Garay, Alfonso. *El palpitar de la casta* (Puebla, 1929).

Lieuwen, Edwin. *Arms and Politics in Latin America* (New York, Praeger, 1960).

Madero, Francisco I. *La sucesión presidencial en 1910* (Paris, C. Bouret, 1908).

Mallory, Walter (ed.). *Political Handbook of the World* (New York, Council of Foreign Relations, 1935).

Manjarrez, Froylán C. *La jornada institucional* (2 vols., Mexico, D.F., 1930).

Mansilla Cortes, José. *Justicia al soldado* (Mexico, 1952).

Martin, Percy. *Mexico in the Twentieth Century* (London, Arnold, 1907).

Meyer, Michael. *Mexican Rebel: Pascual Orozo and The Mexican Revolution, 1910-1915* (Lincoln, University of Nebraska Press, 1967).

Mijares Palencia, José. *El gobierno mejicano* (Mexico, D.F., 1936).

Monroy Durán, Luis. *El último caudillo* (Mexico, D.F., 1924).

Moreno, Daniel. *Los hombres de la revolución* (Mexico, D.F., 1960).

Naranjo, Francisco. *Diccionario biográfico revolucionario* (Mexico, D.F., 1935).

Obregón, Alvaro. *Ocho mil kilometros en campaña* (Paris, C. Bouret, 1917).

Palavacini, Felix. *Historia de la constitución de 1917.* (2 vols., Mexico, D.F., 1938).

Portes Gil, Emilio. *Quince años de política mexicana* (Mexico, D.F., 1941).

Prewitt, Virginia. *Reportage on Mexico* (New York, Dutton, 1941).

Puente, Ramón. *Hombres de la revolución: Obregón* (Los Angeles, 1933).

Quirk, Robert. *The Mexican Revolution, 1914-1915: the Convention of Aguscalientes* (Bloomington, Indiana University Press, 1960).

Quiros Martínez, Roberto. *Abelardo L. Rodríguez* (Mexico, D.F., 1934).

Quiros Martínez, Roberto. Alvaro Obregón (Mexico, D.F., 1928).

Ross, Stanley R. *Francisco I. Madero: Apostle of Mexican Democracy* (New York, Columbia University Press, 1955).

Ruvalcaba, Luis N. (ed.). *Campaña política del Alvaro Obregón, 1919-1920. Compilación de documentos* (Mexico, D.F., 1923).

Salazar, Rosendo. *Del militarismo al civilismo en México* (Mexico, D.F., 1936).

Scott, Robert. *Mexican Government in Transition* (Urbana, University of Illinois Press, 1959).

Silva Herzog, Jesús. *Un ensayo sobre la revolución mejicana* (Mexico, D.F., 1946).

Sorel, Georges, *Reflection of Violence* (New York, Crowell-Collier, 1961).

Tannenbaum, Frank. *Mexico: the Struggle for Peace and Bread* (New York, Knopf, 1950).

Tarracena, Alfonso. *Mi vida en el vertigo de la revolución méjicana* (Mexico, D.F., 1960).

Townshend, William C. *Lázaro Cárdenas* (Ann Arbor, University of Michigan Press, 1952).

Tucker, William P. *The Mexican Government Today* (Minneapolis, University of Minnesota Press, 1957).

Vasquez Gómez, Francisco. *Memorias políticas* (Mexico, D.F., 1933).

Vera Estañol, Jorge. *La revolución mejicana: orígenes y resultados* (Mexico, D.F., 1957).

Wilkie, James W., *The Mexican Revolution: Federal Expenditure and Social Change since 1910* (Berkeley, University of California Press, 1967).

NEWSPAPERS AND PERIODICALS

Boletín Jurídico Militar, 1954.

Diario del Sureste (Mérida, Yucatán), 1937-1939.

Diario de Yucatán, 1948.

El Demócrata, 1925.

Excelsior, 1920-1945.

Gráfico, 1932.

El Heraldo de Mexico, 1920-1923.

Hispanic American Report, 1952-1953.

El Imparcial, 1911.

El Legionario, 1946-1954.

El Liberal, 1914.

Mañana, 1955.

El Monitor Republicano, 1919.

El Nacional, 1931-1957.

New York Times, 1930-1952.

El Popular, 1938.

La Patria, 1926.

La Prensa, 1940.

Revista del Ejército, 1930-1936.

Todo, 1950.

El Universal, 1919-1945.

Washington Post, 1940.

GLOSSARY

academia: academy

alternación: alternation

Aprovisionamientos Militares: Military Supplies

Ateneo de la Juventud: Youth Atheneum

Bando Conservador: conservative party or faction

brigadier: brigadier general

Callista: follower of General Plutarco Elías Calles

cañonazo: cannon ball

Carrancista: followers of Venustiano Carranza

Ciudad Militar: Military City

civilismo: civilianism, i.e., civilian political authority

Colegio Militar: Military Academy

Comisión técnica: technical commission

Comisiones Revisoras de Hojas: Military Records Auditing Commission

Confederación Regional de Obreros Mexicanos (CROM): Regional Confederation of Mexican Workers

Confederación de Trabajadores Mexicanos: Mexican Workers Confederation

constitutionalista: member of Constitutionalist Army

continuismo: continuing in public office beyond one's legal term

conventionistas: those adhering to President Eulalio Guitiérrez

Cristeros: men of Christ

cuartel: barracks

cuartelazo: barracks coup

cuerpos de voluntarios: volunteer corps

Cuerpos Rurales de la Federación: corps of rural irregulars created out of Madero's Ejército Liberatador

defensas sociales: social defense corps

Dirección General de Educacion Militar: Department of Military Education

Dirección General de Materias de Guerra: War Materials Department

divisionario: division general, the highest rank in the Mexican army

Escuelas para Hijos del Ejército: Schools for Army children

Escuela Superior de Guerra: War College

Establecimientos Fabriles: Manufacturing Establishment

Estado Major: General Staff

Ejército Constitutionalista: Constitutionalist Army

Ejército Liberal Constitutionalista: Liberal Constitutionalist Army

Ejército Libertador: Madero's revolutionary army

Ejército Nacional: National army

Ejército Renovador de la Revolución: Reform Army of the Revolution

federales: federals, the regular forces under the Díaz regime

GLOSSARY

Felicistas: supporters of Federal General Felix Díaz

Fondo de Trabajo: Savings fund for work performed

Frente Constitutional Democrático: Democratic Constitutional Front

futurismo: futurism

General de brigada: General of brigade, the 2nd highest rank in the army

generales: generals

Gonzalistas: followers of General Pablo González

guardias blancas: white guards

hacendado: large landholder

imposición: imposition

inspección general: inspector general's office

jefaturas: military districts

jefe de operaciones militares: chief of military operations; commander of a military district

jefe máximo: maximum chief

jefe supremo: supreme commander

jefes: majors and colonels

leva: draft

macho: manly

Maderistas: supporters of Francisco I. Madero

militarismo: militarism

Obregonistas: followers of General Alvaro Obregón

oficiales: lieutenants and captains

Orozquistas: followers of Pascual Orozco

Partido Laborista Mexicana: Mexican Labor Party

Partido Liberal Constitutionalista: Liberal Constitutionalist Party

Partido Nacional Revolucionario: National Revolutionary Party

Partido Revolucionario de Unificación Nacional: Revolutionary National Unification Party

peones: peons, peasants

personalismo: personalism

presidenciables: those eligible to be considered seriously as candidates for the presidency

Primer Jefe: commanding officer

renovador: reformer

rurales: mounted rural constabulary under the Díaz administration

Servicio de Intendencia: Fiscal Management Service

Sexenio: period of six years

soldaderas: female soldiers

subteniente: sub-lieutenant

Vanguardia Nacionalista: Nationalist Vanguard

Villistas: followers of General Pancho Villa

Zapatisas: followers of Emiliano Zapata

INDEX

187

reelection, 96; land reform, 107;
mentioned, 31
Contreras, Manuel J., 65
Corona del Rosal, Alfonso, 145-148
Cosío Robelo, Francisco, 69
Coss, Francisco: civilians in government,
28; *divisionario,* 70; Frente Consti-
tucional Democrático, 128; PRAC,
130; founded National Party of Public
Salvation, 133; mentioned, 75
Council of Sonora, 128
Cristeros, 83-85, 95
CROM (see Confederación Regional
Obrera Mexicana)
Cruz, Roberto: *divisionario,* 88; mil-
lionaire, 92; backed by CROM, 103;
mentioned, 50, 53, 63
CTM (see Confederación Trabajadores
Mexicanos)
Cuernavaca, 99, 109
Cuerpos Rurales de la Federación, 12, 22
Culebra, Rubén, 65
Cumberland, Charles, 14, 16

Defense Ministry, 144
de la Barra, Francisco, 12, 13, 14
de la Huerta, Adolfo: Consul General
in New York City, 50; interim
presidency, 61; Treasury Minister
under Obregón, 74; Plan of Veracruz,
77; mentioned, 29, 53, 78, 79, 81, 86
de la Huerta, Alfonso, 75
de la Rosa, Hector, 52
Departmento de Establecimientos
Fabriles y Aprovisionamientos
Militares, 47
Departmento del Estado Mayor (Gen-
eral Staff Department), 47
Department of Engineers, 111
Department of Military Factories, 120
Depósito de Jefes y Oficiales (Trust of
Chiefs and Officers), 2, 46
Diario de Yucatán, 90
Díaz, Felix, 15, 16, 20, 35, 62
Díaz, Porfirio: ambitious generals, 1-2;
Military Academy established, 3-4;

economic development, 5-6; and
army, 12; and Madero's revolution,
19; War Ministry budgets, 69;
mentioned, 7, 8, 9, 11, 33, 43, 45, 55,
61, 64, 87, 90, 92
Díaz Ordaz, Gustavo, 146
Diéguez, Manuel: *divisionario,* 50;
death, 78; mentioned, 32, 33, 52, 53,
54, 62, 69, 74, 77
Dirección General de Educación
Militar, 110
Dirección General de Materias de
Guerra, 111

Edwards, Lyford P., 7
Eguía Lis, Rafael, 28
Ejército Constitucionalista (see Con-
stitutionalist Army)
Ejército Liberal Constitucionalista
(Liberal Constitutionalist Army), 53
Ejército Libertador, 8, 10, 13
Ejército Nacional (see National Army)
Ejército Renovador de la Revolución,
103
Elizondo, José V., 64
El Nacional, 110
Enríquez, Ignacio C., 37, 54
Ensenada, 91
Escobar, J. Gonzalo, 54, 88, 91, 101, 103
Escobar Rebellion, 104, 105
Escuela Militar de Aviación, 147
Escuela Superior de Guerra (War
College), 111, 147
Escuelas para Hijos del Ejército, 119
Estación Esperanza, 77
Estado Mayor General (General
Staff), 93
Estrada, Enrique, 69, 73, 75, 77, 78

Federal Army: doubled under Madero,
15; formal surrender, 23, 29; mentioned, 11, 12, 14, 16, 18, 19, 20, 21,
22, 35, 36, 37, 59, 84
Federal District, 54, 59
Federation of People's Parties
(FPP), 145

INDEX

INDEX

OAS (see Organization of American States)

Obregón, Alvaro: Treaty of Teoloyucán, 24; occupation of Mexico City, 28-29; tactical superiority, 34; *divisionario*, 40; War Minister, 45; reorganized National Army, 46; Plan of Agua Prieta, 53-54; popular choice for president, 55; civilian, military, and political background, 57-61; assumed presidency, 1920, 62; relations with generals, 64-65; bandits, 66; army reduction, 67-68; War Ministry budget, 69; political activity of army, 71; army professionalism, 71-72; rebellion of December, 1923, 72-78; Organic Law for the Army, 79; wealth, 91; Colegio Militar, 92; Serrano, 96; presidency for second term, 98-99; assassination, 100; mentioned, 7, 20, 21, 22, 30, 31, 33, 38, 43, 47, 48, 50, 51, 52, 63, 81, 82, 83, 87, 88, 90, 103, 108, 118, 120, 132

Organic Law for the Army, 79

Organic Law of 1926, 86

Organization of American States (OAS), 145

Orozco, Pascual: uprising in Chihuahua, 14-15; mentioned, 6, 9, 16, 21, 33, 51, 58, 81, 134

Ortega, Anatolio B., 79

Ortega, Melchor, 117

Ortiz, Eulogio, 92, 104

Ortiz Rubio, Pascual: ambassador to Brazil, 103; president, 1930-1932, 104; cabinet, 106; mentioned, 54, 61, 66, 105, 107, 108, 134

Padilla, Ezekiel, 144

Palavicini, Felix, 42

PAN (see Party of National Action)

Pani, Alberto J., 92

Papacy, 85

Parker, (U. S. Consular Agent), 40

Partido Laborista Mexicano, 133

Partido Liberal Constitucionalista, 73

Partido Nacional Revolucionario (PRN): founded by Calles, 1928, 102; Portes Gil, Cárdenas, presidents, 107; *El Nacional*, 110; reorganization by Cárdenas, 123; replaced by PRM, 125; mentioned, 103, 105, 106, 109, 113, 114, 115, 116, 117

Partido Revolucionario de Unificación Nacional (PRUN), 134, 135, 136

Party of National Action (PAN), 144, 146

Party of the Mexican Revolution (PRM): organization, 125-127; election of 1939, 130-131; renamed PRI, 1945, 144; mentioned, 128, 133, 134, 135

Pelaez, Manuel, 35, 39

Pérez Treviño, Manuel: *divisionario*, 101; Minister of Agriculture under Ortiz Rubio, 107; head of PRN, 114; Anti-Communist Revolutionary Party, 128-129; mentioned, 102, 105, 109, 132

Pershing, John J., 34

Pesqueira, Ignacio, 50, 53

Pineda, Alberto, 54

Plan Felicista, 15

Plan of Agua Prieta, 53, 54

Plan of Ayala, 14

Plan of Guadalupe, 29

Plan of Guaymas, 106

Plan of Hermosillo, 103

Plan of Oaxaca, 77

Plan of San Luis Potosí, 8, 12, 13, 15

Plan Sexenial Militar, 118

Plan of Veracruz, 77

PNR (see Partido Nacional Revolucionario)

Popular Party, 145

Portes Gil, Emilio: "Caudillism," 72; president, 1928-1930, 86; Gobernación Minister, 92; provisional president after Calles, 101-102; head of PNR, 116; mentioned, 104, 105, 106

PRAC (see Anti-Communist Revolutionary Party)

PRI (see Institutional Revolutionary Party)

INDEX

193

INDEX